I.O. Evans Studies
in the Philosophy and Criticism of Literature
ISSN 0271-9061
Number Fourteen

Essays on
Fantastic Literature

by

Brian Stableford

BORGO PRESS / WILDSIDE PRESS

www.wildsidepress.com

Copyright © 1974, 1976, 1981, 1984, 1989, 1995 by Brian Stableford

All rights reserved.
No part of this book may be reproduced in any
form without the expressed written consent of the publisher. Printed in the United States of America by Van
Volumes, Ltd. Cover design by Highpoint Type & Graphics.

Library of Congress Cataloging-in-Publication Data

Stableford, Brian M.
  Opening minds : essays on fantastic literature / by Brian Stableford.
    p. cm. — (I.O. Evans studies in the philosophy and criticism of literature, ISSN 0271-9061 ; no. 14)
  Includes bibliographical references and index.
  ISBN 0-89370-303-6 (cloth). — ISBN 0-89370-403-2 (pbk.)
  1. Fantastic literature—History and criticism. I. Title. II. Series: I.O. Evans studies in the philosophy & criticism of literature ; no. 14.
PN3435.S83 1995   95-5020
809'.915—dc20   CIP

SECOND PRINTING

CONTENTS

About Brian Stableford   4
Introduction   5

1. SF: The Nature of the Medium   9
2. William Wilson's Prospectus for Science-Fiction, 1851   15
3. Opening Minds   23
4. Science Fiction and the Mythology of Progress   29
5. The Concept of Mind in Science Fiction   37
6. The Mythology of Man-Made Catastrophe   53
7. The Plausibility of the Impossible   91
8. Marxism, Science Fiction, and the Poverty of Prophecy: Some Comparisons and Contrasts   99
9. Future Wars, 1890-1950   111

Notes   135
Selected Bibliography   138
Index   139

ABOUT BRIAN STABLEFORD

BRIAN MICHAEL STABLEFORD was born in Yorkshire in 1948. He taught at the University of Reading for many years, but is now a fulltime writer. He has written many science-fiction and fantasy novels, most recently *The Empire of Fear*, *The Werewolves of London*, and *The Angel of Pain*. He has also contributed hundreds of biographical and critical articles to reference books on science fiction, fantasy, and horror, including both editions of *The Encyclopedia of Science Fiction*. His doctoral thesis was published by Borgo Press in 1987 as *The Sociology of Science Fiction*. Other Borgo Press publications by Stableford include: *Algebraic Fantasies and Realistic Romances: More Masters of Science Fiction* (1995); *Firefly: A Novel of the Far Future* (1994); *Masters of Science Fiction: Essays on Six Science Fiction Authors* (1981); and *A Clash of Symbols: The Triumph of James Blish* (1979). Forthcoming in 1995 is *Outside the Human Aquarium: Masters of Science Fiction*, a second, expanded edition of his 1981 publication.

INTRODUCTION

Although my first published essay on science fiction appeared in the same issue of *Science Fantasy* (November 1965) as my first published short story, I did not begin writing such essays in earnest until the early 1970s.

Early in 1972 I was reaching the final stages of an experiment in population dynamics which was supposed to form the basis of a doctoral thesis to be presented at the University of York. The experiment had been running for two and one half years, and I had to count the animals concerned (flour beetles of the species *Tribolium confusum*) every seventy-two hours; it is perhaps understandable that I had begun to entertain doubts as to whether I wanted to spend the rest of my life running similar experiments.

After a period in the doldrums my SF writing had recently taken a leap forward when Don Wollheim bought two novels for DAW, and seemed willing to take more on a regular basis. I thought I ought to give full-time writing a try. Because it seemed prudent to keep my options open, however, I stayed on at the university, transferring to the Sociology Department with the intention of adapting the computer models I had developed for animal population studies for use in human demography. Unfortunately, the department's demographer got a new job immediately before I started and was not replaced, so I decided that I would work on the sociology of science fiction instead. Thus was begun the eccentric process of exploration whose early phases are mapped out in this collection.

While casting around for appropriate theoretical resources, I wrote a number of essays attempting to apply the insights of various books I had read to the analysis of science fiction. My essays on "Schizoid Science Fiction" (based on Anthony Storr's *The Dynamics of Creation*) and "The Transcendental Voyage in Science Fiction" (based on R. D. Laing's then-trendy, *The Politics of Experience*) never reached print, but "SF: The Nature of the Medium," based on the work of Marshall McLuhan, was the second of two pieces I sold to Ted White's *Amazing Stories*; it appeared in the August 1974 issue. In much the same way that selling my first short story had encouraged me with the hopeful illusion that a living might be made from such activity, these sales—no matter that the rewards involved were trivial—helped to convince me that there might be a career of sorts to be built in this way.

OPENING MINDS, BY BRIAN STABLEFORD

"William Wilson's Prospectus for Science Fiction, 1851" was the first of many articles I wrote for *Foundation*, the only British academic journal devoted to the study of science fiction. It was written in 1975 and appeared in *Foundation* no. 10 (June 1976). By this time I had completed three years in sociology, but I had no intention of taking time out from my professional writing to write a thesis. Unfortunately, Britain was then experiencing the first of a series of economic recessions which were to devastate its publishing industry, and a number of books I had written to commission were aborted by the publishers. I was extremely fortunate to excape the resultant financial crisis when I was offered a temporary job at the University of Reading, covering for the sociologist of literature, who was on sabbatical leave. While there I wrote "Opening Minds," which appeared in the British Science Fiction Association magazine, *Vector*, in issue no. 76/77 (August/September 1976). "The Concept of Mind" was written at about the same time for presentation at a conference on "Psychology and Science Fiction" held at Newcastle Polytechnic; this is the first time it has appeared in print.

When my temporary appointment ended, I moved to Swansea and settled down once again to be a full-time writer. I wrote "Science Fiction and the Mythology of Progress" in 1977 at the request of a US fanzine editor, who then rejected it for being "too dry and academic"; it appeared many years later in *Social Biology and Human Affairs* (Vol. 49, no. 2, 1984). Late in 1977, another post fell vacant in the Sociology Department at Reading and I was invited to apply for it; it seemed too good an offer to pass up, so I did—and thus embarked (for a while) on an academic career. I belatedly wrote up my doctoral thesis on *The Sociology of Science Fiction* (Borgo Press, 1987), and began producing academic essays in some profusion. "The Mythology of Man-Made Catastrophe" was written in 1980 for a book called *The End of the World*, edited by Eric Rabkin, Martin H. Greenberg, and Joseph P. Olander (Southern Illinois University Press, 1983), but appeared in the meantime in *Foundation* no. 22 (June 1981). A short version of "Future Wars, 1890-1950" was read at a conference hosted by the "Centre for the Study of Metaphor" at the University of Nice in 1983, and the full version was published in the Centre's journal, *Métaphores* no. 9-10 (Avril 1984). "Marxism, Science Fiction, and the Poverty of Prophecy" appeared in *Foundation* no. 22 (November 1984).

In 1988, during a bout of what any reasonable person would surely regard as insanity, I gave up my tenured post at the university (together with the salary and the pension) to go back to full-time writing. I continue to write the occasional academic article even though there is no earthly point in so doing—"The Plausability of the Impossible" was read at the International Conference on the Fantastic in the Arts at Fort Lauderdale in 1989, and was published in *Foundation* no. 46 (Autumn 1989)—so I suppose there is no reason to be optimistic about the prospect of my eventual recovery from this insanity.

INTRODUCTION

What might I have become, I cannot help but wonder, if I had only stuck to counting flour beetles?

—Brian Stableford
Reading, Berkshire
January 1995

I.

SF: THE NATURE OF THE MEDIUM

Let us first consider the question: what is a medium?

Human beings use media because they are not telepathic. There is no direct way that a man can transfer the content of another man's mind into his own, or convey the content of his own to another. In order that communication may take place at all a medium of some kind must be employed. One primary medium developed by man was speech. In this process ideas are translated into phonemes, transmitted as sound waves, and re-translated into ideas by the recipient. The information-carrying capacity of the medium is very high, but it is not absolute. Not all ideas can be conveyed by speech.

Writing is a secondary medium developed from speech. It is a further translation of speech into new symbols. The *content* of writing is speech, but again we observe that a certain information-carrying capacity is "lost in translation." In making speech into writing, meanings conveyed by tone and emphasis are partly lost. Print is a medium whose content is writing. Print is much more *like* writing than writing is like speech, and the loss of information-carrying capacity is not nearly so great. But print lacks the *character* of writing, and loses that capacity for expression. The use of italics to indicate stress is virtually all that remains of the emphatic capabilities of the written word.

These elementary observations help to point out certain "rules" which apply to the relationship between media. The cardinal rule, formulated by Marshall McLuhan, is that *the content of a medium is always another medium*. The corollary to this is the rule that a medium, in containing another, always loses something of the information-carrying capacity of the contained medium.

There are, however, other observations yet to be made. The fact that writing cannot carry as much information as speech does not mean that it is less *useful* as a medium. By virtue of the manner in which it contains speech, writing gains several new properties as a medium which speech lacks. Writing is portable, whereas speech is not. Writing is long-lasting, whereas speech is not. Writing permits dissociation of transmitter and receiver. It allows the spatial sorting of data—classification and indexing. It can be combined with other media (pictorial) much more easily.

The translation of writing into print involves a small loss in information capacity but a fairly considerable gain in the properties of the medium. It increases the speed of reading and the generalization of the activity. The mass production of the printed book encourages the use of print as a data store and takes a certain burden off the memory by providing it with *reference* books. The standardization of printed characters is a further step in the dissociation of writer and reader.

We can, therefore. add a second corollary rule to that previously deduced: that a medium, in the manner by which it contains another, gains new potential in terms of social usage.

In order to relate these principles to literary media, and SF in particular, we merely have to extend our "genealogy of media" two extra steps. Whether it is legitimate to take these steps is debatable, but let us—in a spirit of experimentation—try. Fiction is a medium whose content is print. SF is a medium whose content is fiction.

In order that we may see more clearly the relationship between SF and "mainstream fiction," let us first look at the relationship between fiction and its own "parent medium," print. The essential property of print which makes it useful is ease of access and usage, promoting data storage facilities. Fiction, in containing print, uses the *modelling* capacity of the language. The function of fiction is not geared to the storage of information, but to the organization of certain types of information into coherent models of reality. The evolution of the literary medium from the print medium establishes a particular ability for data *processing*. The use of fiction is not so much a matter of factual reference as a matter of social reference. Literature makes use of the speed of assimilation characteristic of its contained print medium in building whole *patterns* of information rather than unitary blocks. This a much more complex form of data organization than simple classification. Culture (in both the general and the special sense) can be embodied in literature and communicated by literature.

What, then, is SF? Clearly, more specialized media evolving from the general spectrum of "fiction," losing some of the overall information-carrying capacity of the whole literary medium, may develop in either of two ways: they may feature a special method of processing data, or a method of processing special data. We may assume that the treatment of specialized data will encourage the use of specialized methods, and therefore the second alternative includes the first. The reverse is not necessarily true: special methods of handling data do not necessarily restrict the data. (We may perceive in this distinction something of the special relationship of "content" and "form.")

SF falls into the second of these categories in that it deals with a specific kind of data. The essential property of SF is not so much its characteristic content, but the way people regard it (and thus, perhaps, the way they use it). This consists primarily in the insistence (not necessarily true) that SF features a special (extrapolative) way of processing special (hypothetical and science-connected) data.

At one time, the SF establishment tended to concentrate on a very narrow range of data, defined by the so-called "hard sciences" (physics, chemistry, and biology). Lately, however, the range of data has extended through the "softer" sciences (psychology, sociology, linguistics, anthropology, etc.). Nevertheless, it remains the field of data which restricts SF relative to its contained medium. The extrapolative method is only the method appropriate to the consideration of the role played by this field of data in a social context.

What, then, does SF lose relative to its parent medium, and what does it gain by virtue of its specialization? In terms of information-carrying capacity it is fairly obvious what SF loses relative to literature as a whole. Literature provides a whole "social reference book"—a kind of "ideative handbook" identifying key themes in the culture of a particular time. In the main, however, its concerns are the immediately present and the temporally enduring. SF, with a much narrower field of vision, is able to concentrate first and foremost on those aspects of culture which are immanent and constantly changing.

Critics of SF whose perspective is defined solely by literary consideration seem to think that SF should aspire to fulfill all the functions and potentials of "literature." This is ludicrous. If SF did that it would no longer *be* SF. The literary critic might, perhaps, regard the death of SF as an independent medium as a "progressive" step. I cannot agree—in terms of the development of media it would be a decidedly *retrogressive* step. There is a perspective from which it appears that literature "contains" science fiction and that science fiction could be redissolved within it. But if we regard literature and SF as media, exactly the reverse is true. Science fiction contains, and therefore *constrains* literature. This does not mean that SF is a "lesser" medium than literature, somehow inferior to the so-called "mainstream."

SF, in discarding a large part of the range of literary activity, becomes particularly and specifically applicable to a certain *context* of social reference: the context which extends beyond the present into the future.

The development of SF from general fiction hinges on the same property of print as the evolution of literature from its parent—it is the *speed* of assimilation which enables the medium to transmit patterns which are extended in time rather than in temporally defined space.

So what?

Well, for one thing, if we accept that SF is an intrinsically different medium from the medium which it contains, then criticism of SF on the grounds of whether it is "good literature" or "bad literature" becomes virtually redundant. "Good" (*i.e.*, useful) SF will undoubtedly have certain things in common with "good" (useful) literature, but they are not and can never be the same thing. It is a gross error to assume that the necessary critical tools for the study of SF are already extant in those used for the study of general literature. We cannot judge SF purely and simply by "literary standards."

Similarly, we must not assume that all the methods evolved by the mainstream and by other literary *genres* for the handling of their data are automatically applicable to the special requirements of SF. Conversely, techniques successful in SF will not necessarily be useful in the mainstream. "Bad" literary techniques are not necessarily "bad" SF techniques. "Good" literary techniques will not necessarily produce "good" SF.

There has long been a current of opinion within the SF establishment that anything done by the practitioners of "real literature" can only improve the quality of SF if it is imitated within the medium. This is just not so. (At the same time, it is patently ridiculous to oppose experimentation in narrative strategy and modes of presentation. Without experiment the true potential of the medium cannot be explored. The danger lies in the attitude that experimental results in the mainstream hold good for SF.)

If we accept that the key property of print which permits the "evolutionary chain" of print—literature—SF is the speed of processing and the corollary ease of perception, then it must surely be obvious that techniques which do not facilitate perception and understanding within the special contexts of SF will not be readily adaptable to the medium. Many techniques evolved in the mainstream increase the *density* of data, relying on its familiarity to enhance pattern-perception. SF deals with data which are fundamentally exotic, and simplicity of organization cannot be so readily disposed of.

McLuhan defines media as "artificial extensions of sensory experience." SF extends only part of the range of sensory experience which is the concern of literature, but it extends it in a different direction—a direction which is defined more by the temporal dimension than the spatial ones—and in our attempts to "improve" SF we must remain aware of this crucial difference between the media.

It is at least worth pondering the allegation that the campaign to have SF "accepted as literature" is a waste of time. Indeed, it is possible that the notion of literature as an *élite* cultural medium is out of date. We have witnessed the recent evolution of a whole host of new media, *all* of which are handling and organizing data, and all of which not only represent culture in the widest possible sense, but *are* culture in the widest possible sense. In the final analysis *what* we communicate and the *ways* we communicate define what we are.

In an age when many of our most powerful media have not evolved from print the book is bound to lose its monopoly on culture. It will not become obsolete, but its role will change. In the words of McLuhan: "Print would seem to have lost much of its monopoly as a channel of information, but it has acquired new interest as a tool in the training of perception."[1]

Perhaps this is how we should define science fiction's role in contemporary society: as a "tool in the training of perception." Recent trends in science fiction may offer testimony to the fact that this is the way in which science fiction is evolving. SF has "overflowed" its literary medium. There has been a lateral evolution of SF, so that it contains not only literature, but also cinema, TV, and comics. The academic medium, which contains literature as well as many other media, is now expanding to contain SF. Not all academic studies of SF are based in literary departments.

It is possible that the SF establishment might gain in self-awareness and discover a better chance of increasing the esteem in which it is held by the public if its members were not so ready to accept the role of third-rate purveyors of a "literary culture" which is already past its time. The quest to "define" an entity called "science fiction" within such a literary culture is really quite futile. The treatment of the text as an object complete in itself, as the literary critics have us believe that it is, serves only to obscure the fact that both writer and reader are using the medium to ends which are in no way divorced from the fabric of everyday life. It is not the information passing through the medium which is of primary interest, but the way the information is used by the participants (which depends partly on the way it is organized by the writer and partly on the way it is understood by the reader). We cannot define SF—we can only describe it, and no amount of pontificating on the part of the literary critics can ultimately change or conceal the fact that different people may use SF in different ways.

It is interesting to note that although the progressive development of media along the path mapped herein has tended to the ever-greater dissociation of sender and recipient, there has been a partial reversal of this trend by SF readers and writers. SF has developed a distinct "community," which puts its information organizers (writers), transmitters (editors and publishers), and recipients (readers) in closer contact than the participants in any other print-descended medium. This community has been called a "ghetto" and has been heavily criticized for inhibiting the development of science fiction. Certainly it has helped to remove the medium from the literary mainstream, but I wonder whether this is altogether a bad thing.

It is not difficult, in the social climate of the present day, to discover a need for tools which train perception in the manner of SF. The acceleration of change in the twentieth century has made it clear that "the future" is no longer something our grandchildren will have to live with. It will arrive while we are still around to experience it. We cannot afford to remain willfully blind to the possibilities of the present. Ever since the atom bomb (or, more accurately, ever since the atom bomb was seen to be coming) all men are not only mortal, but exterminable. We all stand to be immediately affected by the decisions and actions of other men. In a global village, there is no place to hide. We can no longer take the future for granted.

II.

WILLIAM WILSON'S PROSPECTUS FOR SCIENCE-FICTION, 1851

> We hope it will not be long before we may have other works of Science-Fiction, as we believe such works likely to fulfil a good purpose, and create an interest, where, unhappily, science alone might fail.[1]

This paragraph contains the first reference to Science Fiction, so far as I am aware, in literary history. The words are those of William Wilson, in *A Little Earnest Book Upon a Great Old Subject*, which was published in 1851.

The "great old subject" of the title is Poetry, and the book consists of Wilson's reflections on that subject, compiled during his summer holiday in 1850.

For the most part, Wilson's thoughts on poets and poetry in general are commonplace and stereotyped. A devout Christian, he considers poetry to be divinely inspired and the highest endeavor of civilized man. There are in the book, however, two chapters which deal with "the Poetry of Science," and in these chapters Wilson breaks original ground, incidentally providing a prospectus for a new literary genre. Seventy-five years were to pass before science fiction was described and labelled a second time by Hugo Gernsback, and it is most interesting to compare Wilson's idea about what science fiction ought to be with the fiction that Gernsback promoted.

Wilson states:

> The Poetry of Science is beginning to attract a considerable increase of attention, and it is most just that it should be so; for the Natural and Mechanical Sciences are alike loaded with rich and wonderful Poetry: Poetry which only requires the clear eyes of the Poet's calm and lofty soul to be perceived and appreciated, and then to be translated palpably by him to the general mind, through the instrumentality of his divine art.

Opening Minds, by Brian Stableford

All known Sciences contain within themselves Worlds of exquisite Poetry, and the more the general mind becomes familiarized with the ever-varying interest and fascinations connected with their Study, the more rapid will become the diffusion and the rise of Science.

Those Sciences which appear to us to be most attractive to the imagination, and to present the widest and best revealed fields of investigation, and to contain even to a surface-inspection of their wonders, their beauties and their combinations—the most Poetry, are the studies of the Philosophical Naturalist, the Botanist, the Geologist, the Astronomer, and the Chemist. The Study and extraction of Poetry from these sciences is like reading mighty books of Life, Beauty and Divinity. But we can only obtain in the end, even if we spend a life in abstract Scientific studies "a cloud-reflection of the vast Unseen."

With what an advance of interest over that of ordinary men must the Man of Science wander in the Fields and the Woods, and traverse over mountains, seas and deserts. The Trees and the Flowers have tongues for him, and the Rivers and the Streams have a History. He knows that the smallest insect, as well as the mightiest animal, has a direct parentage. He knows where the Zoophytes merge into one another: he knows not only the form and colour of a Flower, but the combinations that produce its symmetry and lovely hue: and he knows the laws by which the white sunbeam is thrown back from its surface in coloured rays. He knows, O wondrous fact! "that the dew-drop which glistens on the Flower, that the tear which trembles on the eyelid, holds *locked in its transparent cells* an amount of electric fire equal to that which is discharged during a storm from a thundercloud." Here is Poetry! He knows that *minute insects* have built whole islands of coral reefs up into light from the low deep bed of the vast ocean. Here is Poetry! He knows that neither Matter nor Mind ever die; and that if the fixed laws of Attraction and Repulsion were for one instant disturbed, the whole physical Creation would fall back that moment into Chaos, and that the ponderous Globe itself would then and there evanish.

WILLIAM WILSON'S PROSPECTUS FOR SCIENCE-FICTION

We must overlook here certain errors as regards Wilson's understanding of the scientific knowledge of 1851, and we must look beyond the purple prose at the ideas which he is trying to convey. It is clear that what Wilson is talking about here is a "sense of wonder." It is not quite the same sense of wonder which the science fiction fan talks about, being wonder inspired by knowledge rather than imaginative possibilities, but it has a good deal in common with it. The quotation within the quotation is attributed by Wilson to "Hunt's *Poetry of Science*"—a title which I have been unable to trace—which he seems to have read at some point in the summer holiday during which he was recording his thoughts. This sense of wonder has been awakened in Wilson by the revelation that scientific knowledge may permit a man to see the world through different eyes: eyes informed of the true complexity of the natural world. It has been revealed to him that there is detail in the world about us which is inaccessible to our senses, that singular events may have a deeper significance in terms of the scientific principles which lie behind them.

It was apparently not Hunt's *Poetry of Science* alone which brought this home to him, for he goes on to make the following observations:

> Fiction has lately been chosen as a means of familiarizing science in one single case only, but with great success. It is by the celebrated dramatic Poet, R. H. Horne, and is entitled "The Poor Artist; or, Seven Eye-sights and one object."[2]

This is followed by the sentence which I quoted at the beginning of the esssy. Critics and literary historians have offered many candidates for the dubious distinction of being the first work of science fiction, but *The Poor Artist* is conspicuous by its absence from their lists of the genre's seminal works. (It is, perhaps, a little remarkable that Wilson should identify this as the "single case only" of fiction presenting a scientific perspective, but it is possible that he was not conversant with the work of Poe, who had died the previous year, and highly probable that he had not come across Mrs. Griffith's *Three Hundred Years Hence*—which he might not, in any case, have considered "lately" enough.) However, though *The Poor Artist*, like Wilson's commentary on it, has been overlooked by the new critics of SF, it is not without interest. Here is Wilson's description of it:

> The story of "The Poor Artist" is in itself—although only used as a garb in which to make "the revelations of a reasoning imagination" appear the more attractive—full of earnest and speculative interest. The story of a high, simple, true spirit, struggling

with unalterable will and determination towards an ennobling purpose, is pleasingly told.

He does good work who leads us thus seductively, along the pleasant road of fiction, to such thought-inducing glimpses of the "Poetry of Science" as we find here. The different aspects in which any one given object may and must appear to each differently formed insect and animal vision is the cause of the six sketches taken by the Poor Artist from descriptions given to him by a Bee, an Ant, a Spider, a Perch, a Robin, and a Cat. On investigating the object itself, he finds that the whole six have seen on the grass a shining golden sovereign, covered with bright dew-drops, and that his six strange pictures, all entirely different, of this single object, have been caused by the *different sights* of each of the little narrators. This little book, however, does not stop here; many thought-digressions spring from the contemplation of creation's unrevealed wonders.

The Poor Artist is a story of revelation, and there is no coincidence at all in the fact that it deals with the same revelation which had already seized Wilson's imagination thanks to Hunt's *Poetry of Science*. Here again, we have the innocent sense of wonder at the knowledge that what our eyes tell us is neither the whole truth nor the only truth. This description of *The Poor Artist* puts one very much in mind of J. B. S. Haldane's essay, "Possible Worlds," in which Haldane attempts to describe the world-view of the barnacle, and concludes with the oft-quoted remark that "the world is not only queerer than we imagine, but queerer than we *can* imagine."

It is worth noting also how similar to Gernsback Wilson sounds in his account of this story. Gernsback, in his editorial to the first issue of *Amazing Stories*, spoke of science fiction as "charming romance intermingled with scientific fact and prophetic vision," and this was very much how he saw it—to him, the story was just a vehicle for the speculation: "only used as a garb in which to make 'the revelations of a reasoning imagination' more attractive." It is clear that the science fiction which Wilson is trying to describe is the same science fiction which Gernsback was later to define, not the science fiction of later, more sophisticated definitions. Wilson goes on to say:

> Campbell says that "Fiction in Poetry is not the reverse of truth, but her soft and enchanting resemblance." Now this applies especially to Science-Fiction, *in which the revealed truths of Science may be*

WILLIAM WILSON'S PROSPECTUS FOR SCIENCE-FICTION

given, interwoven with a pleasing story which may itself be poetical and *true*—thus circulating a knowledge of the Poetry of Science, clothed in a garb of the Poetry of life.

The italics here are mine (except for the word "true"), and they emphasize a phrase that might just as well have been written by Gernsback. Indeed, Gernsback—again in his editorial to the first issue of *Amazing*—spoke of Poe and Verne in almost exactly this way; he referred to "amazing romances, cleverly interwoven with a scientific thread."

It is significant that Wilson, having made these points about the potential of science fiction, should himself be drawn into the realms of scientific speculation. Perhaps it is almost inevitable that having discovered a sense of wonder in the perspectives of science, one should then be carried away by it. It is certainly a natural step, for as Wilson notes of *The Poor Artist*, "this little book does not stop here; many thought-digressions spring from the contemplation of creation's unrevealed wonders."

The first of his speculations concerns animal languages and the injustice of the phrase, "dumb animals." Not only does he suggest that the audible noises made by familiar animals may communicate information, but he also argues for the possibility that apparently voiceless animals may communicate using sounds outside the range of human hearing.

He writes:

We know that when we gaze at some beautiful ruin, the space between our eye and the object is full of numerous tribes of living insects. We know that the very air which we breathe, and the water which we drink, both are also full of life. Is it not, then, as reasonable to suppose, that if life which we cannot see exists everywhere around us, so languages which we cannot hear, and which if we could hear, we could not of course understand, are spoken around us, by animals and insects which we consider to lack the power of sound.

Lest this argument appear rather too reckless to his readers, Wilson then proceeds to marvel—again, exactly as Gernsback was to marvel seventy-five years later—at the great achievements already to be credited to modern science.

The modern discoveries and applications of Science throw deeply into the shade the old romances and fanciful legends of our boyhood. The Arabian Nights' Entertainments—The Child's Fairy Tales—Oberon and Titania—The Child's Own Book—all are robbed of their old wonder by the many marvels of modern Science. The Magnetic Needle—which has grown into the almost Omnipresent Electric Telegraph—has more magic about its *reality*, than the wildest creations of child-fiction and legend have in their *ideality*. The Fairies never fancied anything more wonderful than holding conversations thousands of miles apart, and they only effected such things in Story; yet such conversations are now every-day commonplaces. It really does not seem out of the way to look forward to the day—and that day not far distant—when the Mother Country may thus hold hourly communication with her various gigantic Colonial Infants in each hemisphere of the Globe.

The Electric Telegraph, when calmly thought of—and when we consider that the full powers of Electricity are not yet developed—is certainly the most wonderful of the modern applications of the discoveries of Science; because—as we have observed before—it almost realises in the mind Omnipresence! Truly, to the thoughtful mind, the days of Miracles are not over.

We will only make passing mention of frequent ascents in great Nassau Balloons, filled with 90,000 feet of gas, and travelling many miles above the Earth's surface across the Channel in the night, and landing in the morning somewhere in the far South of France.

We will only make passing mention of the entire banishment of night, as it were, from our great cities—by means of the soon-to-be-used Electric light—which, at a given hour, or even moment, will suddenly illuminate whole towns with a brightness almost equal to the light of day.

We will bestow but a glancing word upon Britannia Tubular Bridges—monster trains conveying thousands of passengers at the rate of sixty miles per hour and the joining of the Atlantic and Pacific Oceans. We are sure, however, of one fact; that not many generations ago, to *talk* of such noble achievements would have resulted in confinement for life as a lunatic, and to have been successful in one or other would have been deemed a miracle. Many things that science has rendered common often approach sublimity.

The Amputation of Limbs without pain, the abstraction and replacement of eyes without the knowledge of the owner, are no longer things of even common surprise.

This was written twelve years before Jules Verne published the first of his *Voyages Extraordinaires*—and thirty-seven years before Edison actually perfected the electric light bulb which Wilson foresaw illuminating cities by night at the flick of a switch. It is significant that priority of place in this catalogue of wonders is given to the telegraph—a breakthrough in communications—for it was, of course, the invention and development of its successor, radio, which so inspired and involved Gernsback. It is the use of Science in facilitating *communication* which is of paramount importance to Wilson: in the communication of perspectives which allow people to see the world in a different light, and in making it easier for people to communicate with one another. The telegraph destroyed distance in making communication easier, but Wilson also looked to Science to overcome failure to communicate of a different kind. He looked to the human sciences to allow people to gain a better understanding of one another, and perhaps it is forgivable that his enthusiasm carries him away in this respect (as, in fact, similar enthusiasm carried away other speculative thinkers in more recent times) and makes him a champion of a plausible pseudo-science. In Wilson's case, it is Phrenology, but it is quite clear from his expectations of Phrenology—his motives for embracing it—that his is the same enthusiasm which led men with similar minds to embrace ESP, Dianetics, and General Semantics.

Wilson writes:

What power over his fellow men is possessed by him who understands it, and how often in his passage through life may it not save him from imposition, miscalculation of impulse, and the many pangs of false friendship, and deceived love, and the bitter sorrows that thickly spring from misreposed confidence....The Statesman, and especially the Diplomatist, would often find that such a science, well used, might be turned to the vast advantage of whole Nations and Races....Thus the Poetry of Phrenology rests in its Great power of good; it may be made, if justly used by a true man, a Peacemaker, a Guide, and a Consolation.

Opening Minds, by Brian Stableford

L. Ron Hubbard, science fiction writer turned prophet, claimed no more (and no less) for his own custom-designed science/religion.

The fact that it was William Wilson, and not Hugo Gernsback, who invented the idea of science fiction is little more than a footnote for the historians intent on making a publishing category into a literary corpus with its own self-contained historicity. But there is something much more important to be learned from the pages of *A Little Earnest Book Upon a Great Old Subject* than the mere fact of Wilson's priority, and that is the manner in which the idea originated—the reason why the idea came to him and interested him. The "Poetry of Science," the business of scientific speculation, and the notion of science fiction as an intellectual and artistic discipline, are all bound up with the realization (perhaps easy enough today, but not so easy in the intellectual climate of 1850) that the world we see is only a very small fraction of the world that is, and that in getting to know more about the world that is we may learn a great deal more about the world we see, and thus about ourselves. This is the revelation that common sense is often misleading, and that what is obvious is not necessarily true.

Wilson's prospectus for science fiction was ignored, and has been forgotten. In 1851 it was ahead of its time. But the intellectual discovery made by Wilson and dramatized by Horne was to be made again and again over the next seventy-five years, in many areas of scientific thought. James Clerk Maxwell discovered that the light we see is only a tiny fraction of a vast electromagnetic spectrum. Bohr and Einstein revealed that the world of the atom is a world of mathematics/abstractions where common sense concepts do not hold good. Hubble and Shapley discovered the vastness of the universe beyond the limits of visibility. William Wilson's revelation was confirmed in no uncertain terms by science. Perhaps it would not be too bold to argue that the rediscovery of Wilson's prospectus, in virtually identical form, during the early years of the twentieth century was historically inevitable.

III.

OPENING MINDS

The purpose of this article is to compare and contrast two different approaches to the art of science fiction (and by "the art of science fiction" I mean not simply the art of science fiction writing, but the whole art of science fiction thinking, which is the prerogative of readers as well as writers).   The best way to compare these approaches, I think, is to look at the methods and the work of two men who used and developed them in the same historical period: H. G. Wells and Alfred Jarry.

Wells was born in 1866, Jarry in 1873, the former in England and the latter in France. Their early writings appeared in the mid-1890s. There is a certain similarity in their educational and vocational background: each hesitated at one time between a career in science and a career in literature, and each opted for the latter. Their work converged at one point, when Jarry was inspired by Wells's novel *The Time Machine* to write a speculative article on "How to Construct a Time Machine," presenting a different concept of the nature of time.

Wells studied under Thomas Henry Huxley, the English evolutionist who was the most prominent champion of Darwinism. Jarry studied under the French evolutionist, Henri Bergson, who became one of the principal opponents of Huxley's interpretation of Darwin's theory. In this curious biographical parallel we may find the source of the intellectual division which resulted in the works of Wells and Jarry (though both wrote what might loosely be termed "science fiction") being poles apart.

Huxley was a "hard" Darwinist, determined that the harshness and cruelty of "the struggle for existence" and the "survival of the fittest" must be accepted as the rule of life, from which men could not be immune. He believed these principles to have been blessed by scientific proof, and thus canonized as scientific truth. Bergson, on the other hand, was concerned with fitting the ideas of Darwinism into a natural philosophy much more general in kind—he saw Darwinian theory as no more than a model, reduced in value because it could not take its place in a greater metaphysical schema.

Wells, pupil of Huxley, became a proponent of what is now termed "hard" science fiction. His works were scientific not only in their content but in the method of their composition. He adopted simple hypotheses and attempted to trace by rigorous logic their implications for man, society, and the world. Usually, he permitted no more than one such hypothesis per story, and he did his best to make it seem reasonable, fitting it into the scheme of the story as plausibly as possible.

In the introduction to the definitive collection of his longer scientific romances (collected by Victor Gollancz in 1933), Wells wrote that "the writer of fantastic stories...must help [the reader] in every possible way to *domesticate* the impossible hypothesis. He must trick him into an unwary concession to some plausible assumption and get on with his story while the illusion holds." This is the method behind *The Time Machine*, *The War of the Worlds*, *The Island of Dr. Moreau*, and *The Invisible Man*, and it is very successful—these works are quasi-realistic, and the reader will accept their initial premises easily. In later works, like *The First Men in the Moon*, more ambitious hypotheses prove a little harder to swallow, but the method remains the same, and the attempt is there.

Wells thus held the highest priority in his speculative work to be the *rational* development of hypotheses and their *plausible* presentation to the reader. He took his inspiration from the idea of the scientist as a steadfast seeker of truth, dedicated to the classical scientific method of hypothesis and experiment, and the rigorous testing of notions.

Jarry, however, drew his inspiration from a different kind of scientist, from men to whom scientific thought was an adventure, who produced new ideas in quantity: explorers in the imagination. Bergson was one such, and so was Clerk Maxwell, who revolutionized physics with his synthesis of electromagnetism and a new theory of light. Maxwell was not so much an experimenter in the laboratory or in the field as an experimenter in the mind. In order to make his kinetic theory of gases comprehensible, he imagined a "demon" which, by selecting appropriate molecules, could engineer the transfer of energy from a cool gas to a hot one. No such demon could exist, and perhaps it was irreverent to imagine him, but the idea helped the mind to grasp the logic of Maxwell's theory.

There were nineteenth-century scientists who were both adventurers in the imagination and rigorous experimenters (Poincaré, Lord Kelvin, and even Edison), but for the most part the dichotomy reflected by Wells and Jarry was a real one. Maxwell predicted the existence of electromagnetic waves in the ether, but could not demonstrate their presence. Hertz, after years in the laboratory, found the waves, but lacked the imagination to see their potential in wireless telegraphy (radio).

Jarry wrote two "neo-scientific novels" which bear very little resemblance indeed—on a superficial level—to Wells's scientific romances. In *The Supermale*, investigating the possibilities of men becoming more than men, Jarry featured a race between a five-man bicycle team fed on "superfood" and an express train, while another character gives evidence of the benefits to be gained by an ascetic training in performing erotic feats of an amazing nature. The second novel, *The Exploits and Opinions of Dr. Faustroll, Pataphysician*, is completely disordered—a chaotic mass of ideative inspirations drawn from scientific texts and symbolist poetry, a surreal celebration of bizarre philosophical concepts. Wells's hypotheses are there in profusion—dramatized (often melodramatized) but never organized or rationally developed. The very last thing Jarry would have considered doing to a new idea was "domesticating" it.

Jarry is remembered today not so much for his *avant-la-lettre* science fiction, but for a short story called "The Crucifixion of Christ Considered as an Uphill Bicycle Race" (whose title is—amazingly enough—self-explanatory), and for his dramatic work. He was the pioneer of the "theatre of the absurd," which he developed through his magnificently vulgar character, Papa Ubu. Ubu appeared for the first time on the Paris stage in *Ubu Roi*, which begins with his shouting obscenities at the audience. Jarry's explanation of the philosophy of his compositions was that if theatre audiences were to be presented with the spectacle of characters like themselves acting out mundane and eminently sensible scripts, then all the commonplace illusions to which they were already committed would be made even firmer. He wanted to make people open their minds, to shock them out of their mental strait jackets and offer them new opportunities to think. He wrote of allowing audiences the "relief" of seeing on the stage that which they did *not* understand, and the "active pleasure" of participating in the ideative explorations of the playwright. His science fiction, too, is intended to jolt dull minds into new paths of thought.

In the service of these ideals, Jarry invented a whole new science: pataphysics, the "science of imaginary solutions." He wrote:

> Pataphysics will examine the laws governing exceptions, and will explain the universe supplementary to this one; or, less ambitiously, will describe a universe which can be—and perhaps should be—envisaged in the place of the traditional universe, since the laws that are supposed to have been discovered in the traditional universe are also correlations of exceptions, albeit more frequent ones.

(Here again, incidentally, we can draw a parallel between Jarry and Wells, for Wells's first important piece of scientific journalism, "The Rediscovery of the Unique," pointed out that technology made available the means of measuring minute differences among apparently similar phenomena, thus affirming the uniqueness of all entities and all events.)

Opening Minds, by Brian Stableford

One foundation stone of Jarry's philosophy of science was the notion of "clinamen"—a concept introduced by Titus Lucretius into *De Rerum Natura*, his popularization of the atomic theory of Democritus and Epicurus. Clinamen is supposedly a tiny swerve in the motion of an atom, entirely at the discretion of chance, which is the hypothetical "ultimate cause" of all events and phenomena. Kelvin had resurrected the idea of clinamen for his own theory of matter, and it is curiously similar to the notion of "uncertainty" imported into modern scientific doctrine by Heisenberg. This "chance swerve"—the irrational origin of all rational behavior of matter—is reflected in Jarry's work by the chance swerving of the mind from idea to idea, making imaginative leaps and settling nowhere.

Jarry died in 1907, aged thirty-four. Wells lived to be eighty. Such fame as Jarry achieved was local and short-lived (although he has been "rediscovered"), whereas Wells became universally respected in his own lifetime as a philosopher and writer.

Modern science fiction, through its critics and its writers, still pays homage to Wells. Few of them have even heard of Jarry. And yet even the most cursory glance at contemporary science fiction declares that Jarry's methods survive, alongside those of Wells.

The modern writers of "hard" science fiction—almost all graduates of the Campbell school—take their brief from Wells. Writers like Isaac Asimov, Arthur C. Clarke, Poul Anderson, and Hal Clement pose their hypotheses, and pursue the implications thereof with ruthless discipline. Those who have written critical manifestos championing this kind of science fiction (Heinlein, Blish, and others) stress the *realistic* qualities of SF, its determination to stay within bounds of scientific possibility. All imaginative exercises which fail this rigorous standard are relegated to the status of "fantasies."

There are, however, writers like R. A. Lafferty, Harlan Ellison, A. E. van Vogt, Philip K. Dick, and Barrington J. Bayley, who still consider that what they are involved with is science fiction, and yet make nonsense of the Wellsian standard. The discipline of the classical scientific method is in no way represented in their work. They are adventurers among ideas, and—whether they are aware of it or not—they are the intellectual descendants of Alfred Jarry. Clinamen plays an important role in their thinking and their art, and their effect on the reader is to jolt his mind into new and unforeseen paths. These writers, too, have their champions among critics who have written manifestos for science fiction (Alexei Panshin belongs to this group, as did the prophets of the so-called "New Wave" era), declaring that science fiction is a form of fantasy whose business is to disturb settled routines of thought, and whose claim to scientific fidelity is both spurious and unnecessary.

In a sense, it is a pity that this polarity should still exist today. Many science fiction writers—particularly those of real ability—can work in the one mode as well as the other (and this includes some of the writers whose work I instanced as exemplary of one mode or the other).

The polarity between Wells and Jarry was an opposition within a basic similarity. Wells and Jarry were both involved in the business of opening minds, and were opposites only in that they had very different ideas as to how minds might be opened.

Wells's idea was that minds should be opened by the merest crack, so that a new idea might be slipped in without the mind fully realizing that its boundaries had been breached. Once inside, the idea might then interact with the contents of the mind to expand its imaginative horizons. Wells, and Wellsian science fiction, attempts to invade the mind a little at a time, introducing new ideas one by one, and in such a way that they may not seem too alien. It is a cunning method (but by no means dishonest).

Jarry scorned such cunning and he had no patience with careful procedures. His intention was to dynamite the boundaries of the mind, sweeping them away with a great flood of ideas. His policy was one of confrontation and challenge—overt and dramatic (and in no way dishonest).

There can be no doubt that Wells's method worked better at the turn of the century, and probably works better today. The cunning, diplomatic way is more successful—minds often react to the Jarryesque confrontation by closing up completely. The fact that one method is relatively more successful does not, however, mean that Wells was "right" and Jarry "wrong." It should be noted that in twentieth-century science it is the experimenters in thought (Maxwell, Einstein, Dirac) who are remembered as men of genius—for they it was who assaulted old dogmas with daring new concepts. These are the scientists Jarry would have admired. It should also be noted that the reason that these men can be hailed as geniuses is that other men (Hertz, Eddington, and Carl Anderson) did the experimental work which proved them right. *These* are the scientists Wells admired. There is no progress without thinkers of *both* kinds. Someone has to create new ideas, and someone has to test them—and it is a simple fact that only a very few men have the temperament to do both. One might almost suggest that science fiction writers are especially favored, in that there seem to be a considerable number of them who are capable of marrying Wellsian methods to Jarryesque extravagance.

It is, I think, inevitable that science fiction writers should have discovered and used Jarryesque methods, without even knowing of his example, for it is through the methods of Jarry that the Wellsian imagination is provided fuel. It is perhaps also inevitable that it should be the Wellsian methods which are most revered within the field, while the Jarryesque are less respectable. Wellsian philosophy is, after all, *tried* and *tested*, guaranteed by classical scientific methodology, while Jarryesque exploration is irrational, irreverent, and mercurial.

OPENING MINDS, BY BRIAN STABLEFORD

We should, I think, be prepared to recognize the kinship between Wells and Jarry, and we should not be so determined to define boundaries between their methods. Clinamen has its part to play, in science as well as in the imagination; it has a role in the generation of the hypotheses which are to be tested by the rigors of scientific knowledge, and it has a more intimate function to fulfill in challenging the limits of imaginative elasticity, in taunting and mocking the security of our ideative frameworks. No one who aspires to an open mind (as, surely, all readers of science fiction must) can afford to dismiss the fruits of pataphysics as uninteresting or inconsiderable.

IV.

SCIENCE FICTION AND THE MYTHOLOGY OF PROGRESS

The word "progress" was originally a common noun meaning a journey. It was not until the seventeenth century that it slowly began to accumulate special overtones. John Bunyan's allegory, *The Pilgrim's Progress*, represents in its title an intermediate stage in the evolution of the word. Here its trivial meaning is overlaid with other implications. The journey here is *life*'s journey, with its special goal. Most important of all, the pilgrim's progress is a process of *improvement*. By the early eighteenth century, the notion of improvement had been built into the meaning of the word. Edward Young could write, in 1742:

> Nature delights in progress; in advance
> From worse to better; but when minds ascend,
> Progress, in part, depends upon themselves.

This echoes Bunyan well enough—the progress of the individual, his *spiritual* progress, is seen as a process of self-improvement. The word rapidly found another connotation, however, not in reference to human individuals but to the human race as a whole. People began to talk of *history* as a pattern of progress: as a gradual process of improvement, of *civilization*. Previously, history had been construed as a pattern of events, arbitrarily determined by the actions of individuals, without any inbuilt *process*, even though its ultimate destiny might be predetermined. Now, the story of mankind came to be seen as one of steady advance towards enlightenment. The motor of this process of improvement was held to be knowledge, and the very substance of the change was the advancement of science and reason. To the sages of western Europe it seemed obvious that their societies were changing, and that freedom and justice for all men were flowering as the inevitable consequence of the process of change. Reason was remaking social relationships and forms of government. The following was written by the French philosopher Turgot in 1750:

> Manners are gradually softened, the human mind takes enlightenment, separate nations draw nearer to

> each other, commerce and policy connect at last all the parts of the globe, and the total mass of the human race...marches always, although slowly, towards still higher perfection.

At first these theorists worked within the limits of a static psychology: they believed that human society was changing but that human nature was not. Subsequently, however, the tide of optimism brought forth the notion that even man himself was progressing, and that human nature was perfectible. This was the prospect held out to their fellow men by such philosophers as William Godwin and the Marquis de Condorcet. The latter proposed that:

> Nature has set no term to the perfection of human faculties...the perfectibility of man is truly infinite; and...the progress of this perfectibility, from now on independent of any power that might wish to halt it, has no other limit than the duration of the globe upon which nature has cast us.

Ideas such as these were the fuel that animated the American and French revolutions. There were, of course, dissenters from the optimistic spirit: Rousseau thought that the spiritual nature of modern, civilized man was degraded and demoralized relative to the noble savage, while Malthus was pessimistic about the perfectibility of human society because of the tendency of populations to increase so as to outstrip their resources, but the idea of progress dominated the social philosophy of the day.

In the mid-nineteenth century Karl Marx and Friedrich Engels suggested that the engine of history—the agent which moved society through its stages of improvement—was not knowledge *per se*, but rather the development of the means of production available to various cultures. In this view, it was not so much what men *knew* that determined their progress, but what they could *do*. This transferred the emphasis from science to technology—but what was meant by progress was still *social* and moral progress for all that the argument was couched in materialistic terms.

Other historians and social theorists of the nineteenth century, however, were responsible for a gradual de-emphasizing of the notion of moral perfectibility and the moral and spiritual aspects of human progress. The influence of the Darwinian theory of evolution, which took the teleological emphasis out of evolutionary philosophy, was an important factor in encouraging such historians as Bagehot to accentuate the fitness of societies, their material wealth, and their potency in environmental control. However, it was not social Darwinism alone that accounted for the trend, which is also evident in the work of Buckle, who published his work before the advent of *The Origin of Species*.

Gradually, in the nineteenth century, materialism took over the mythology of progress, until by the turn of the century it was possible to draw a contrast between material/technological progress and moral progress. Some Utopian socialists, such Edward Bellamy—author of the best-selling *Looking Backward*—considered the two to be interdependent, but others dissented from this view. In *News from Nowhere*, his famous reply to *Looking Backward*, William Morris claimed that our hopes for the social and moral improvement of mankind could only be fulfilled if the advance of technology were to be halted, and the grip of the industrial revolution upon the pattern of history deliberately relaxed. Much of the social philosophy of H. G. Wells, manifested both in his fiction and his non-fiction, is intensely preoccupied with analyzing the relationships between technological progress and the social and spiritual progress of mankind. By the end of his life, when he wrote *Mind at the End of its Tether*, he had despaired of ever solving the problem, and was convinced that all hope of progress was gone, and that the human species was doomed. The mythology of progress had by this time entered an entirely new era.

Science fiction is the principal literary byproduct of the mythology of progress. It is, in today's world, the principal "shop-window" in which that mythology is displayed. Its history bears eloquent testimony to the changes which have overtaken that mythology in recent times. Hugo Gernsback, introducing the notion of "scientifiction" in the first issue of *Amazing Stories*, said confidently of the stories that would be written for the magazine that "Posterity will point to them as having blazed a trail, not only in literature and fiction, but progress as well."

Gernsback followed Bellamy in believing that the social and moral progress of mankind were determined by technological progress, and that more powerful machines were both necessary and sufficient to assure the development of a better society. The same assumption was held by many of the writers whose work he promoted in his early magazines—notably the German Utopian writer, Otfrid von Hanstein. Of the early stories written specifically for Gernsback, Lilith Lorraine's "Into the 28th Century"[1] provides a perfect example of this attitude. Less optimistic writers than these were not prepared to accept that the advancement of technology was a sufficient condition of the development of a better world, but the dominant opinion was that it would help.

There were emerging, however, other points of view which developed more pessimistic arguments to the effect that increases in technological achievement, far from paving the way to a better world, actually posed a threat to social and moral improvement. A number of

OPENING MINDS, BY BRIAN STABLEFORD

writers became steadily more eloquent and more prominent in continuing the tradition of Rousseau and William Morris, seeing civilization and mechanization as demoralizing, and potentially dehumanizing, patterns of development.

Basically, there were two lines of argument advancing this intellectual cause. Firstly, there was the suggestion that as men came to rely more and more upon the power of their machines their own personal abilities would decline, so that their culture would stagnate and degenerate. Eventually, needing to invest no personal effort in the struggle to survive, they would become idle and purposeless lotus eaters. One of the most striking early representations of this notion is E. M. Forster's classic short story, "The Machine Stops." The idea came into magazine science fiction in the early thirties, most memorably in "Twilight" by John W. Campbell, Jr. writing as "Don A. Stuart." The most sophisticated literary development of the theme is perhaps to be found in Kurt Vonnegut's first novel, *Player Piano*.

The second line of argument promoting the view that technological progress is inimical to the development of a better society is one that was stated particularly eloquently by Bertrand Russell in the twenties, in an essay entitled "Icarus; or, the Future of Science." Here, Russell argues that technology gives power to existing power-groups, and that as technology advances, so will these power-groups be better equipped to oppress their fellow men and secure their power. Thus, the advance of science promotes and facilitates tyranny. The classic literary developments of this line of thought are Aldous Huxley's *Brave New World* and George Orwell's *Nineteen Eighty-Four*. It became particularly noticeable in magazine science fiction after the war, when the advent of the atom bomb gave governments the power to destroy the world. A particularly neat exemplification of the arguments can be found in T. L. Sherred's story, "E for Effort."

The new antipathy toward the particular version of the myth of progress that Gernsback—operating in the tradition of Marx and the social Darwinists—espoused grew steadily within science fiction through the forties, and accelerated rapidly in the post-Hiroshima decade. It did not, however, sweep away the opposition. Its main effect was not to destroy the mythology of progress but to force it through a series of metamorphoses which dramatically altered its main emphases. In a sense, in fact, what the new lines of argument did was to force the mythology of progress to revert to its older modes of thought, recovering in some measure the attitudes of the eighteenth century.

Two main trends are visible in the optimistic progress mythology of postwar science fiction. The first is a new emphasis on *knowledge* rather than technology. The main grounds for the defense of scientific and technological progress were no longer an appeal to the *power* of environmental control which it would give to men, but an appeal to the capacity of science and technology to open up new horizons

SCIENCE FICTION AND THE MYTHOLOGY OF PROGESS

and new opportunities. The proposition that technological progress would create tyranny on Earth was met and cancelled out by the proposition that it would also provide the means of escape from these tyrannies in the shape of spaceships which would carry men to new worlds. This pattern of argument is especially evident in such novels as *The Space Merchants* by Frederik Pohl and Cyril M. Kornbluth, and *The End of Eternity* by Isaac Asimov.

The second main trend which reaffirmed faith in progress while sidestepping the anti-technological arguments was the heavy postwar emphasis on superhuman evolution. Here there was a total reversion to the notion of progress as primarily a matter of *spiritual* progress, completely independent of technological advancement. Such supermen as Wilmar H. Shiras's *Children of the Atom* are clearly the morally and intellectually perfectible beings envisioned by the Marquis de Condorcet. Theodore Sturgeon's *More Than Human*, especially in its third section, is very much preoccupied with the notion of moral perfectibility. Arthur C. Clarke's *Childhood's End* provides a particularly striking example of the new humanistic emphasis in that it is the work of an extremely outspoken apologist for technology. A particularly forthright statement of this line of thinking is to be found in Clifford D. Simak's novel *Ring Around the Sun*, in which a group of superhuman mutants set out to save ordinary mankind by transporting them into a series of alternate Earths where they can live an idyllic pastoral existence:

> The mutants would take from the human race the deadly playthings and keep them in trust until the child of Man was old enough to use them without hurting himself or injuring his neighbor....And the culture of the future, under mutant guidance, would be not merely a mechanistic culture, but a social and an economic and an artistic and spiritual culture as well as mechanical. The mutants would take lopsided Man and mold him into balance....

The "deadly playthings" mentioned here are, of course, the products of technological progress.

Contemporary science fiction differs sharply from the bulk of prewar magazine science fiction because it has recovered the belief that the kind of progress which really *counts* is social and moral progress, and because it takes a far more critical and open-minded attitude to the question of how social and moral progress are related to the advancement of technology. Contemporary science fiction testifies to the fact that it is now very difficult to accept technological progress as an *encouragement* to social and moral progress, let alone a necessary and sufficient condition of it.

OPENING MINDS, BY BRIAN STABLEFORD

The most eloquent apologists for technological advance, notably Clarke and Asimov, have had to work hard in their recent work even to argue the case that technological advancement does no injury to the cause of social and moral progress. Optimism in contemporary science fiction has two main loci: the hope that we can achieve some kind of synthesis between technologies and spiritual progress; and the hope that if we cannot, then we can progress spiritually to transcend in some way our dependence upon technology. Where modern SF writers deal in tragedy, they feature the negation of these hopes.

Not all theories of history, of course, have been progressive ones. There have been several philosophers of history who have reacted against the idea that there is in the story of man some implicit process of improvement. What *they* have seen in the story is rather a cyclic process in which all growth is followed by decay, and nothing endures. This is, of course, a much older view of human affairs than the mythology of progress itself, but it became unfashionable in the wake of the Enlightenment. Its most eloquent modern proponents have been Oswald Spengler and Arnold Toynbee (though Toynbee modified his pessimism as his work developed). Both saw the present phase of western civilization as one of decline rather than of advancement, and both saw the future as a matter of the decay and gradual obliteration of western culture. This mode of thought, too, is represented in some measure in modern science fiction. James Blish exploited both the pessimistic and optimistic potential of Spengler in his *Cities in Flight* series, dealing with the birth of a new culture as well as the death of the old. The book that is perhaps the most pessimistic of all the recent products of the speculative imagination—Thomas M. Disch's *334*—also refers explicitly to Spengler. Charles L. Harness incorporated views of Toynbee's earlier work into his novel *The Paradox Men*, in which a tyrannical future state brings history to an apocalyptic climax; but more than any other writer Harness has been a promoter of transcendental mythology as a metaphor of spiritual progress, and *The Paradox Men* allows humankind a literally miraculous escape from its historical predicament. Nor is Disch's pessimism completely unrelenting, for another of his novels—*Camp Concentration*—features a similar miracle.

In modern science fiction there are many apocalyptic visions which see our contemporary situation as a bad one getting worse. The argument which Malthus used against Godwin reappeared in science fiction in the sixties, in such novels as Harry Harrison's *Make Room! Make Room!* and John Brunner's *Stand on Zanzibar*. To the notion of population crisis there was rapidly added the hypothesis that society might be poisoned by technology's wastes, a view put forward forcibly in Brunner's *The Sheep Look Up* and Philip Wylie's *The End of the Dream*. These dark visions are, however, frequently balanced out by a countervailing mythology which suggests that if we cannot overcome these difficulties, we might at least transcend them in some way. This balancing theme is very noticeable in Brunner's work, where the novels mentioned above and the despairing *Total Eclipse* contrast with *The Dreaming Earth*, *The Stardroppers*, and *The Stone That Never Came Down*.

Science fiction is now, as it has always been, a literature in which progress is the principal value. In its history, however, it displays some of the flexibility of meaning which is contained within the word. If its visions of imaginable futures have any real intellectual value it is surely in revealing to us the weaknesses of the crude thinking which lumped together all of the various facets of the mythology of progress. Perhaps, too, they help to reveal the weakness of the mythology of progress itself—the assumption that implicit in processes of change are processes of improvement. It is true that knowledge grows and accumulates, and it is true that as knowledge grows, so does our power over the environment. The belief, however, that this growth of knowledge is sufficient to ensure the improvement of human society and human morality is built on foundations which are logically and empirically insecure.

The postwar science fiction which represents the new mythology of progress, dealing largely in images of superhumanity and transcendent metamorphosis, is—by and large—extremely unrealistic. It cannot pretend, as Gernsback's science fiction could, to follow actual historical trends visible in the real world. Science fiction which *does* deal with social progress (insofar as it is compatible with contemporary historical trends—the work of Mack Reynolds, especially *Looking Backward from the Year 2000* and its sequels, is a good example) is very much a minority activity. It is at least arguable that the merits of science fiction's contemporary mythology of progress are largely allegorical (some of its impressive products, notably Harness's *The Rose* and Robert Silverberg's *Son of Man*, are straightforwardly allegorical). If this is so, then science fiction can no longer pretend to "blaze a trail" in progress, but fulfills the much more modest function of helping us to ask ourselves *what actually counts* as progress.

This is, I think, a function of which we need not be ashamed, and in terms of this function the history of science fiction has not been without its achievements.

V.

THE CONCEPT OF MIND IN SCIENCE FICTION

My purpose in this essay is to explore the ways in which science fiction writers have developed and used various notions of what kind of thing the human mind is and what kind of potential may be implicit within it, though as yet unrealized. I also want to point out certain important changes which have taken place over time in characteristic attitudes to the mind and its possible future evolution, and to say something about why these changes have taken place.

I will begin by quoting from a novel called *The Mortgage on the Brain* by Vincent Harper, which was first published in 1905. It is one of a number of novels which develop in a rather melodramatic fashion the notion of "split personality," and in terms of its literary merits it is quite unexceptional. It is, however, a very interesting novel because of its didactic aspect—it is to some extent a vehicle of propaganda, promoting a particular attitude not only to the specific mental disturbance featured in the plot, but to psychology as a discipline. It speaks, in fact, with the voice of crusading positivism. A foreword to the narrative contains the following declaration:

> Signs are not wanting, that when speculative Science formulates its next hypothesis respecting life, very little will remain of what was formerly looked upon as the exclusive field of the metaphysician and the theologian. Recent revolutionising discoveries having to do with the functions and attributes of matter are fast bridging the chasm between psychology and physics...."Mind" and "thought" and "spirit" are now being tossed into the melting pot of fearless analysis, quite as freely as those other time-honoured "basic facts"—ether, force, and our useful old friend the atom. Out of it all is slowly but surely emerging the idea that ignorance and superstition long ago formed a Mortgage on the Brain of man, which it is high time to repudiate before the bar of reason.

The spokesman for this viewpoint within the novel is the brilliant Dr. Yznaga, one of those figures beloved by historians of science who steadfastly maintain their commitment to truth in the face of vilification and persecution by the champions of theological superstition. The innocent narrator asks him, at one point, about the Ego postulated by metaphysicians as the seat of identity and consciousness, and is told that it does not exist. Yznaga is absolutely certain of this, and waxes lyrical in pursuit of his point:

> "What is this pretender 'Personality' anyhow? What constitutes an 'individual,' I ask? What distinguishes 'me' from 'you?' I will tell you—nay, I will quote your own words, learned sir, in your work on Memory. You there state, that 'personality' is merely the sum total of the cerebral and nervous conditions and capacities found combined within a human being, and played upon by certain external forces. Very well, then, by your own terms you demolish the upstart Ego, since it is not a fixed, personal, spiritual something existing independently of the brain, but merely the transient, constantly changing and always accidental result of the play of external forces upon whatever may be the combination of cerebral and nervous conditions at any given time."

Yznaga is not only a positivist, but also a hardened pragmatist, and his analysis of the consequences of this conceptual mistake is a bitter one. What is more, he is willing to declare that when the truth *is* known and welcomed, and the tyranny of superstition destroyed, then the consequences will be Utopian. When the narrator asks what, in his scheme of things, becomes of moral responsibility, Yznaga replies:

> "You ask what becomes of moral responsibility? I reply, that this present world of misery and horrors would be transformed into a paradise, were it but shown to man that the incandescent fibre within his brain is but his little segment of the one eternal, universal all-life, and that this incandescent fibre—the lamp of consciousness, that is to say—glows bright or dim, gives light or burns out, accordingly as it is adjusted and fitted and cared for and co-ordinated with the demonstrable Best Way. What an ethical regeneration would follow any such conception of the true nature of life! What an unspeakable night of remorse and the tortures of 'conscience' and of memory and of madness would be forever dispelled by the dawning of

THE CONCEPT OF MIND IN SCIENCE FICTION

the new day of rational existence! With what fresh hope the present degenerate, sin-scarred, enfeebled, cringing human race would set about the glorious work of perfecting these brain-bulbs in which the life-current of electricity glows, for our little hour on earth, in what we choose to call man's intellect!"

We may feel that the reference to the "little segment of the one, eternal all-life" is rather too metaphysical to take its place in authentic positivist rhetoric, but this can probably be put down as an overenthusiastic metaphor generated by the fervor of the argument. What is being mounted here is an all-out attack on Cartesian dualism, which is similar in spirit, if not in strategy, to Gilbert Ryle's celebrated attempt to "lay the ghost in the machine." Harper has not the least patience with Descartes's "mental substance" which inhabits the brain, but which is somehow external to it and transcendental of its physical apparatus. *The Mortgage on the Brain* is the most extreme early scientific romance which takes a positivist view of psychology, but it is by no means the only one. Edward Bellamy wrote a novel about a device for obliterating memories, entitled *Dr. Heidenhoff's Process*, which similarly took a soundly pragmatic line in evaluating the utility of such an instrument. A method of photographing memory cells in order to recover visual images is featured in another nineteenth-century novel, *Dr. Berkeley's Discovery* by Richard Slee and Cornelia Atwood Pratt. There are also numerous attempts to document imaginary "case studies" exemplifying particular psychological disorders, two of the earliest being Edgar Fawcett's *The New Nero* and Albert Bigelow Paine's *Mystery of Evelyn Delorme*, the latter involving psychotropic effects similar to those imagined by Stevenson in *Dr. Jekyll and Mr. Hyde*. The tendency of these stories is to accept the brain as a physical system, with no spiritual added extras.

Stories of this type were, however, in competition with others which took a very different line of approach. These other tales supposed that science would very soon find evidence which *endorsed* Cartesian dualism by providing proof of the existence of a non-material psyche inhabiting the material body. Such writers took their imaginative warrant from the physics of Maxwell, particularly the concept of "fields of force," and from the notion of energy in general. Perhaps it is not surprising that the concept of energy should lend itself to being "taken over" by those wishing to conceptualize and describe a non-material persona, in view of the fact that Helmholtz, who introduced the modern concept of energy in his paper "On the Conservation of Force," had been influenced in his thinking by the several years he had spent in Johann Müller's laboratory investigating the possibility of their being some essential "vital force" animating all living creatures. It was in the notion of some "*élan vital*" or "life force" that supporters of Cartesian

39

dualism found their endorsement. There are particularly striking examples of this kind of idea in Camille Flammarion's *Lumen* and Edgar Fawcett's *The Ghost of Guy Thyrle*. The latter novel involves a scientist who discovers a drug which enables him to detach his persona from his physical body, which then remains inanimate, as if dead—a vehicle without a driver.

Marie Corelli decided that Maxwellian physical theory (which she understood very imperfectly) was the key to the understanding of all spiritual phenomena, and in her best-selling novel, *A Romance of Two Worlds*, she imagined God as a ring of pure electric fire, with angels and human souls being sparks generated thereby. Later, after Rutherford and Soddy's experiments with radioactivity, she substituted for this all-electric God a God of pure radiation. The same scientific work gave birth to the notion of permanently-disembodied minds, which later became a convenient way to imagine alien beings. From the very beginning, such imaginary beings were conceived as superior to material creatures, having somehow transcended the vulgar dependence of lesser beings on despicable matter. It was not long before imaginative writers began to wonder whether the evolutionary destiny of mankind might not be a similar triumphant transcendence. This idea provides the climax to George Bernard Shaw's play, *Back to Methuselah*, whose final act is entitled "As Far as Thought Can Reach."

Here we find the She-Ancient commenting: "None of us now believe that all this machinery of flesh and blood is necessary. It dies."

The He-Ancient echoes: "It imprisons us on this petty planet and forbids us to range through the stars."

One of the youths to whom they are talking objects to the notion that mind and body are separable: "But even a vortex is a vortex in something. You can't have a whirlpool without water; and you can't have a vortex without gas, or molecules or atoms or ions or electrons or something, not nothing."

"No," replies the He-Ancient, "the vortex is not the water nor the gas nor the atoms: it is a power over these things."

The She-Ancient adds: "The body was the slave of the vortex; but the slave has become the master; and we must free ourselves from that tyranny. It is this stuff, this flesh and blood and bone and all the rest of it, that is intolerable. Even prehistoric man dreamed of what he called an astral body, and asked who would deliver him from the body of this death."

It is, of course, the view of the ancients which is endorsed by Lilith in the final speech of the play, where she—the progenitor of the evolutionary process—reflects on its accomplishments:

> "They have redeemed themselves from their vileness, and turned away from their sins. Best of all, they are still not satisfied: the impulse I gave them in

The Concept of Mind in Science Fiction

that day when I sundered myself in twain and launched Man and Woman on the earth still urges them: after passing a million goals they press on to the goal of redemption from the flesh, to the vortex freed from matter, to the whirlpool in pure intelligence that, when the world began, was a whirlpool in pure force..."[1]

The published version of *Back to Methuselah* carries a long preface in which Shaw gives his reasons for rejecting the materialist evolutionary philosophy of Darwin and Haeckel, preferring instead Lamarckian metaphysics and the Bergsonian notion of *élan vital*.

These two opposed lines of thought were well-established in imaginative literature before the birth of genre science fiction and the spectacular boom in speculative fiction which followed it. Early magazine SF was, for the most part, rigidly secular in its world-view—it steered clear of ideas which were considered tainted by superstition. One might have expected, therefore, that it was the positivist line of argument exemplified by Harper that would have become established in genre SF as the dominant attitude. In fact, this is not so. The overwhelming majority of science fiction writers, from the earliest days of the SF pulps to the present, have adopted—without, of course, realizing its origins—a Cartesian Dualism re-endorsed with a jargon which refers more-or-less haphazardly to "pure energy," "pure force," and "pure intelligence." While I intend to investigate the reasons for this, it may be as well to digress briefly here to make my own philosophical position clear.

My own opinion has, of course, no relevance to any explanation of the reasons why SF writers in general tend to adopt one of two alternative attitudes, but it is relevant to one further contention which I will make. I argue that if science fiction were, as it sometimes pretends to be, an extrapolative medium which can justify its imaginative extravagances by virtue of their secure foundation in scientific knowledge and theory, then Cartesian Dualism in its cruder versions could have no possible place within it. The fact, therefore, that crude Cartesian Dualism is so common in science fiction as to be virtually conventional helps to reveal the falsity of this pretence. This will come as no surprise to anyone, but my reason for making it explicit is in order to make the point that if we want to try to understand why modern science fiction has the preoccupations which it does have, then the notion of adventurous but conscientious extrapolation from known science will not help us in the least.

The title of this essay echoes the title of Gilbert Ryle's attack on Cartesian Dualism, *The Concept of Mind*. The covert implication that I, too, am not well-disposed toward Cartesian Dualism is intended.

Opening Minds, by Brian Stableford

I should like to say, however, that I am far from being in total agreement with Ryle's position. When we talk about the notion of the ghost in the machine there are many ghosts we might be talking about, and my objection is to what Ernest Gellner has called the "paramechanical ghost"—the ghost which is made of Cartesian "mental substance," and which, despite being immaterial, nonetheless manages to function as a kind of puppet-master pulling the levers which activate and control the central nervous system. Gellner, in commenting on the various versions of the ghost in the machine, wants to save from Ryle's attack that he calls the "warm ghost" of consciousness, while he abandons the cold paramechanical ghost to the slaughter without a pang of conscience. This is what he says on the matter:

> He [the warm ghost] has a role in daily life which is of great interest to philosophy: he is, so to speak, a very plausible candidate for what one can only call our ultimate identity. In states of crisis, when we look with detachment at many of our own traits and aims and assumptions, and are prepared to re-value and possibly reject them, who is that inner self who takes a step back and surveys the scene, including much of the more expendable outworks of the ego, its own past convictions and commitments, and who decides what can be salvaged, is worth salvaging, and where we shall move next? It is of course very difficult to pinpoint this, and much harder still to *justify* the preferential identity, so to speak, of anything that we do locate; and we may also refuse to take at face value the feeling, possibly the illusion, that reflexive consciousness, turning upon itself in a moment of reorientation, really can choose a new course, or has either the independence to make, or the resources to implement, crucial decisions....All the same, my consciousness is at least a plausible candidate for my ultimate identity, and reflective people do fall back on it in crisis or when values are re-valued, and there is some connection between this kind of ego—private conscious reflection—and the purified bundle of sensation acting as evaluator of cognitive claims.
>
> So much for the warm ghost, the stream of consciousness or the bolt-hole of identity. The cold one is only found in works of philosophical psychology, and usually old-fashioned ones at that. He is rather paramechanical, and is invoked to *explain* our various mental capacities. He indulges in activities that usually have names of Latin origin, such as apprehension,

conceptualisation, and so forth. I hold no brief whatsoever for *this* ghost. Explanations in terms of his powers and doings seem to me quite worthless, for various obvious reasons (circularity, absence of direct or indirect observability of the entities invoked in the explanation, sloppy logical connections with the phenomena to be explained)....Ryle's attack on this paramechanical ghost is fully justified.[2]

This commentary, it seems to me, is eminently fair, and I agree with it all, except for the statement that the cold ghost is only found in old-fashioned works of philosophical psychology. Alas, he is not. He also haunts modern science fiction, and has done so throughout its history.

There are several roles in which this paramechanical ghost appears frequently in genre SF. The first is, of course, in connection with evolutionary fantasies, where his role is that given to him by Shaw. Pulp SF has two common images of the future evolution of man, one of which sees that future as a gradual process of physical degeneration, and which takes its key image from Shaw's fellow Fabian, H. G. Wells, who popularized it in his essay on "The Man of the Year Million." This notion of the man of the future is frequently tied in magazine SF to the notion of over-dependence on machines, and is best exemplified by such stories as John W. Campbell Jr.'s classic tale, "Twilight," and Harry Bates's "Alas, All Thinking!" The more optimistic Shavian version of the ultimate evolutionary destiny of mankind is perhaps most memorably represented by Eric Frank Russell's story, "Metamorphosite," in which the apparently-human protagonist trying to avert a galactic war eventually turns out to be wearing his body merely as a matter of temporary convenience; when he finally reveals his true incandescent magnificence, he seems to be an entity of pure radiance. Such eschatological themes tended to disappear from the SF magazines in the postwar period, but disembodied minds produced by extended processes of evolution did not.

Alien beings of this kind crop up regularly, and invariably our relation to them is seen as that of immature infant to fully mature adult, or that of man to God. In James Blish's rather didactic juvenile novel, *The Star Dwellers*, the paternalistic energy-aliens are actually referred to as angels. The fire balloons of Mars, in Ray Bradbury's short story, are a literal religious revelation to the priests who are the story's main human characters. In Arthur C. Clarke's *Against the Fall of Night*, rewritten as *The City and the Stars*, there are two immensely powerful "pure mentalities" whose natures are opposed to one another: one is the benevolent Vanamonde, the other the baleful "Mad Mind." In another Clarke novel, *Childhood's End*, the notion of evolutionary transcendence recurs, though here it is the result of a short-term process rather than billions of years of extended and slow evolution. In this novel a whole generation of Earth's children leave behind their bodily vehicles as they go to fuse with the disembodied "Cosmic Mind." Clarke denies that there is any religious symbolism in this story, though the text itself describes this event as an "apotheosis."

There is no doubt that what is happening in these stories—quite consciously in the case of George Bernard Shaw, apparently unconsciously in the case of Arthur C. Clarke—is no more than a transfiguration of Christian salvation mythology, its plausibility overhauled by means of the conscription of a new jargon. The process is parallel to the attempt made by the French Jesuit Pierre Teilhard de Chardin to recast Catholic theology in a mold shaped by modern evolutionary philosophy. There is more to be said about this, but in the meantime it is necessary to consider some other roles played in SF by paramechanical ghosts.

The second important role played in science fiction stories by paramechanical mind-entities also has an obvious analogue in the traditional repertoire of the supernatural imagination. The analogue is the notion of demonic possession, and its science-fictional versions are nightmarish thrillers in which human beings are "taken over" by alien intelligences, so that they become mere puppets of the forces of evil. Sometimes their own minds remain conscious but helpless, more often their personalities are temporarily or permanently displaced. The ability to do this is one of the talents of the alien vitons who are the owners of the human race in Eric Frank Russell's Fortean fantasy, *Sinister Barrier*, and invasions of Earth are conducted on this basis in such novels as Robert A. Heinlein's *The Puppet Masters*, Murray Leinster's *The Brain Stealers*, and Frank Crisp's *The Ape of London*.

It is worth noting that there are two distinct aspects to the horrific component of such stories as these. One is the horror of the possibility of being taken over oneself—particularly well dramatized in such stories as Robert Silverberg's "Passengers" and Frederik Pohl's "We Programmed People." The other is the horror of not knowing whether the person you recognize as a friend might in fact be a deadly enemy—an anxiety particularly well delineated in John W. Campbell Jr.'s "Who Goes There?" and Jack Finney's *Invasion of the Body-Snatchers*. The latter has been filmed twice, and another film of the same ilk is based on Joseph J. Millard's similar story, *The Gods Hate Kansas*. Some stories in this second group are not take-over stories in the strict sense, but tales in which the aliens build duplicates to replace real people; but the appeal to the emotions of the reader is similar to that found in straightforward stories of alien possession. The origin of the first fear expressed in these stories is easy to appreciate. If, from the viewpoint of Cartesian dualism, I see myself a mechanical body, then the notion of my being displaced by a stronger *persona* is by no means absurd. The second kind of anxiety is to a rather different kind of existential insecurity—the paranoid fear that the familiar and ordinary world might in fact be only a façade concealing implacable hostility, and the uneasy sense that one's interactions with the world may be based upon presuppositions which are woefully inadequate.

There is a particularly interesting variant of this theme, rarely found in modern science fiction but familiar from fantastic literature owing allegiance to the supernatural imagination, and that is the notion of identity-exchange, whereby two minds exchange bodies. Classic stories of this type include Théophile Gautier's novella, "Avatar," Sir Arthur Conan Doyle's story of "The Great Keinplatz Experiment," Edgar Fawcett's *Douglas Duane*, Elleston Trevor's *The Immortal Error*, and J. Russell Warren's *This Mortal Coil*. Of these only the Doyle story puts up any pretence of being science fiction, but there are a number of modern SF stories in which humans—usually unwillingly—exchange bodies with aliens. The two most significant are Damon Knight's satire, *Mind Switch*, and James Tiptree Jr.'s novel, *Up the Walls of the World*. There are also one or two complex stories in which minds hop peripatetically from body to body, usually resulting in awkward confusions, because one is never quite sure, in the most literal sense, who is who. Examples include Robert Sheckley's *Immortality Inc.* and Philip José Farmer's *Traitor to the Living*. Once again, this notion is a perfectly straightforward corollary of Cartesian Dualism. The idea lacks the immediately obvious nightmarish quality of the notion of mental takeover, and this relative lack of dramatic potential explains the fact that it is not so common as a story-device.

Another kind of plot, which might be considered a second variant of the idea of takeover, is that which involves the *sharing* of one body by two (or more) minds. This too has its nightmarish aspect—the notion of being invaded, of having the realm of one's innermost self violated by an alien presence—but in actual fact this nightmarish quality is exploited relatively rarely. Where alien passengers are concerned the relationship is often uneasy, but even when much is made of the uneasiness—as in Leigh Brackett's *Sword of Rhiannon* or my own series of novels begun with *Halcyon Drift*—the results of the meeting of minds are positive ones. Where two human minds are involved, there may be similar attention paid to the difficulties of mutual adjustment, but only in rare cases—Robert Silverberg's *The Second Trip* is the cardinal example—is there outright existential warfare. Silverberg's *To Live Again* takes a much more lenient view of the possibilities of mind-sharing, and there are a number of novels which seem almost to comprise enthusiastic propaganda in favor of it—the best examples are Dave Van Arnam's *Starmind* and Robert A. Heinlein's *I Will Fear No Evil*. Roger Zelazny's *Doorways in the Sand* and Ted White's *By Furies Possessed*, and to a lesser extent Hal Clement's *Needle*, seem almost enthusiastic about the possibilities inherent in human/alien partnerships.

Opening Minds, by Brian Stableford

At first, the positive approach to this kind of idea is very puzzling, as the close affinity between the notion of mind-sharing and the notion of alien possession would seem to make the former only a more dilute version of the latter. When we look more closely at the stories, however, we find that the situation is being interpreted very differently, and rather different concepts are being invoked. Especially helpful in this regard is Ted White's *By Furies Possessed*, which not only concerns itself directly with the analogy with demonic possession, but which is framed as a kind of "ideological reply" to Robert A. Heinlein's *The Puppet Masters*. There is no straightforward mind-sharing in White's novel, but merely an infestation of the body by an alien organism which not only allows the human mind better control over a more healthy body, but also allows a curious kind of "consciousness-raising" to take place. The humans involved construe this as an authentic religious experience, and join together as an organization naming itself "the Church of the Brotherhood of Life." The experience is seen as a kind of symbiosis, and proceeds on the assumption that an association between human and alien can—and *ought to be*—mutually beneficial. It is strongly opposed to the Darwinian logic used by Heinlein to argue that human and alien must necessarily be locked in a struggle for survival which can only end with the annihilation of one species by the other.

One important thing to note is that many of the mind-sharing novels cited, like *By Furies Possessed*, do not operate from within the world-view of Cartesian Dualism. Neither *Doorways in the Sand* nor *Halcyon Drift* assume a dualistic perspective, though I must concede that the latter comes perilously close. However, it is not simply the abandonment of the dualistic perspective (and with it some of the implicit threat of mind-sharing) that is responsible for the more positive attitude. *I Will Fear No Evil* is clearly dualistic, and so is the one positive story of mind-exchange, *Up the Walls of the World*.

This reversal of attitude is partly a historical one. Before the second world war the standard role of the alien being in SF was that of invader of Earth and deadly enemy of humankind. It was in this period that *Sinister Barrier*, *The Brain Stealers*, and *The Gods Hate Kansas* were written. After the war there was a dramatic swing in characteristic attitudes to alien beings and to the possibilities of meeting and communicating with them. Stories of mind-sharing are one dramatic way in which this new positive attitude can be emphasized: symbiosis replaces parasitism and predation as the key concept in human/alien affairs. There is, however, another aspect of the situation which is more evident with respect to those stories concerned with human mind-sharing. Quite apart from the *literal* mind-sharing which appears in *I Will Fear No Evil* and *To Live Again*, in which the minds of dead people are preserved intact in the bodies of living hosts, there is another kind of mind-sharing which has played a very prominent role in postwar SF: the notion of telepathy.

There are several ways to build analogical models or speculative pseudo-theories accounting for telepathy, and not all of them assume a dualistic perspective. Telepathy most commonly appears in SF, however, as part of a kind of "package deal" in which it is thrown together with certain other mental powers, lumped together in the jargon of Professor J. B. Rhine as "psi powers." One of the other powers included in this package deal is psychokinesis, which is perhaps the example par excellence of reasoning by corollary from the assumption of Cartesian Dualism. If I conceive of my mind as being a special substance which has paramechanical power over my material body, it is but a short imaginative step to wondering whether it might not also be able to "reach out" from its home in my head to exercise its paramechanical power over other material objects in my neighborhood. Science fiction stories about psi powers almost invariably use this metaphor of "reaching out" in connection with both psychokinesis *and* telepathy. In particularly obvious stories the notion of a quasi-physical "mental substance" is very obvious indeed. For example, Tom Reamy's *Blind Voices* mentions the psi-powered superman reaching out with mental "fingers" to pinch the arteries of his enemies and give them heart attacks. In Octavia Butler's *Mind of My Mind* the similarly powered heroine and villain literally attach telepathic threads of mind-substance to their less powerful lackeys. The common idea that telepathy is a kind of "mental radio" is no less dualistic when analyzed, and rests upon analogical speculation whereby mental substance is credited with a set of pseudo-energy relations in exactly the same way that ordinary matter is related to ordinary energy.

The immense popularity of psi stories in the postwar period is primarily due to the imaginative utility of the Rhinean account of these powers. If Rhine could be trusted, then there might be thousands of people walking the streets who, without knowing it, actually had latent superpowers which might at any moment blossom into full-blown superhumanity. There is no easier myth to sell than the myth that anyone might secretly be superman—it is the perfect way of pandering to our proclivity for indulging in power-fantasy. The notion that every inoffensive-seeming Clark Kent might really be Superman inside—or, more realistically, might safely play with the fantasy of being Superman—has obvious and almost universal appeal. However, that is not all there is to it, for it is here that we return once again to the concept of burgeoning superhumanity as an important stage in the evolution of mankind. The only difference between the psi-mythology of postwar SF and the evolutionary fantasies already considered is one of time-scale. The last act of *Back to Methuselah* is set in A.D. 31,920, and even then mankind is only partway to its ultimate destiny. The SF stories of the fifties psi-boom were set in *today*, or, at the very latest, tomorrow. In

OPENING MINDS, BY BRIAN STABLEFORD

much the same way that Christian eschatology replaced Jewish eschatology with promises of short-term, cut-rate salvation, so postwar SF went into the marketplace of ideas advertising more-or-less instantaneous transcendence. Earlier, I pointed out that the ideas featured in Arthur C. Clarke's *Childhood's End* are strikingly similar to those in Teilhard de Chardin's *Phenomenon of Man*. The one vital *difference* between them is the envisaged time-scale—and *Childhood's End* is in this matter conservative by comparison with other contemporary SF texts. Such apotheosis-novels as Keith Laumer's *The Infinite Cage* and Oscar Rossiter's *Tetrasomy Two* are set very firmly in the present-day world.

To summarize, we can distinguish several roles played by the paramechanical ghost in modern science fiction. There are several ideas which arise almost by necessity as corollaries of a dualistic perspective, and all of these are represented in modern SF. Some of these notions—especially the idea of mental takeover—are inherently nightmarish. Others—especially the notion of psychokinesis—fit in marvellously well with our most treasured daydreams of power and potency. It need not surprise us that the paramechanical ghost survives within science fiction to serve these functions, and there need be no dispute over the fact that insofar as these kinds of story are concerned, we are dealing with the substance of pure fantasy, not with any serious extrapolative exercise rounded in the theoretical edifices of contemporary science.

There is, however, more to the picture than this brief snapshot—in fact, much more. We are left with the necessity of accounting for the other roles played by the paramechanical ghost, including its commonly-allotted role in human evolution. In particular, we need to explain why, in the postwar years, there was a considerable increase in the use of this kind of role, and why there was imported into this part of the mythology of science fiction a sense of urgency, and very frequently a visionary and propagandistic zeal which pre-empted to a large extent such notions as mind-sharing, largely purging these notions of the nightmarish quality attached to them by virtue of their association with the notion of alien possession.

To help us in our quest for an explanation of these data it is helpful to refer to one of the most famous products of postwar SF—a novel of imminent human evolution and transcendence of the human condition which is not at all a vulgar power-fantasy. It was published in the same year as *Childhood's End* and has much in common with it—*More Than Human* by Theodore Sturgeon. This novel uses the concept of *gestalt* in a rather different application from that of Wertheimer and Köhler, involving the linking of several individual minds into an organized compound whole. The whole has a power and an organization that go far beyond the talents of the individual parts, who—though

THE CONCEPT OF MIND IN SCIENCE FICTION

possessed of one or other of the psi-powers—are disastrous failures as isolated members of humankind.

Much of the narrative is concerned with the way in which they come together and learn to function as a *gestalt* group, but this is only the first part of their program of transcendence. The final section of the book tells how the group learns morality and accepts its responsibility to the rest of humankind. Only then do they find themselves welcomed into a community of similar *gestalts*, entering into a new world of consciousness and communication. This is the dialogue which then takes place, when the spokesman for the story's featured group asks:

> "Are you....we....responsible for all humanity's accomplishments?"
>
> *"No! We share. We are humanity!"*
>
> "Humanity's trying to kill itself."
>
> (A wave of amusement, and a superb confidence, like joy.)
>
> *"Today, this week, it might seem so. But in terms of the history of a race....O new one, atomic war is a ripple on the broad face of the Amazon!"*

Their memories, their projections and computations flooded in to Gerry, until at last he knew their nature and their function; and he knew why the ethos he had learned was too small a concept. For here at last was power which could not corrupt, for such an insight could not be used for its own sake, or against itself. Here was why and how humanity existed, troubled and dynamic, sainted by the trust of its own great destiny. Here was the withheld hand as thousands died, when by their death millions might live. And here too was the guide, the beacon, for such times as humanity might be in danger, here was the Guardian of Whom all humans knew—not an exterior force, nor an awesome Watcher in the sky, but a laughing thing with a human heart and a reverence for its human origins, smelling of sweat and new-turned earth rather than suffused with the pale odor of sanctity.

He saw himself as an atom and his *gestalt* as a molecule. He saw these others as a cell among cells, and he saw in the whole the design of what, with joy, humanity would become.

He felt a rising, choking sense of worship, and recognized it for what it has always been for mankind—self respect.

Opening Minds, by Brian Stableford

He stretched out his arms, and the tears streamed from his strange eyes. *"Thank you,"* he answered them. *"Thank you, thank you."*
And humbly, he joined their company.[3]

There are two aspects of this passage that warrant attention. Firstly, the religious imagery is again clear, and quite explicit. Secondly, what appears to be a digression is, in fact, a vital comment—the reference to humanity's supposed tendency to self-annihilation whose instrument, the atom bomb, is so contemptuously brushed aside by the community of *gestalts* as a thing of no significance.

I believe that it was James Blish, in his essay "Cathedrals in Space," who pointed out the upsurge of interest in religious themes and ideas which began in science fiction in the late forties, and it was he who asserted that the reason for this was an outburst of "chiliastic panic" occasioned by the new consciousness that the end of the world might really be at hand now that men possessed the power to destroy it. The atom bomb created a threat to existential security no less nightmarish for being so utterly impersonal than the sense of insecurity generated by imagining that an alien mind might suppress one's own consciousness and take over one's body.

In many ways the atom bomb set the seal on a suspicion that had been growing since the depression of the thirties, that the myth of social progress was a false one, that no Utopia would arise out of man's technological mastery of the environment, and that the history of the twentieth century was to be a matter of things getting worse instead of better. We are all, today, perfectly familiar with that suspicion, and most of us probably take it for granted in our everyday lives. As SF readers we are all perfectly aware of what the effect of this has been on futuristic speculation. There has been a massive swing away from Utopian optimism, so that the great majority of contemporary stories of the future work on the assumption that a historical and political solution to our present predicament is virtually out of the question. There has been a massive displacement of optimism and hope, so that upbeat stories which accentuate the positive aspects of future possibility have been forced to find new loci for their enthusiasm. They have found them in a new mythology of human evolution, in ecological mysticism, and in new attitudes to the concept of alien intelligence. These new foci, particularly and most emphatically the first, but also to some extent the third, have encouraged a resurgence of interest in the human mind, much of which—though not quite all—covertly adopts the imaginative framework of crude Cartesian Dualism.

The consequence of the considerable shift in the vocabulary of symbols used to evoke an optimistic sense of future possibilities has been that science fiction has in recent decades become far less realistic and far more fantastic. However naive the Utopian schemes of early twentieth-century writers may seem today, the writers were at least dealing with the prospects for political action in the real world. They pinned their hopes to the ordinary endeavors of human beings, and used the miracles of science and pseudoscience sparingly. The naivety of postwar writers is not so obvious, and is often partially masked by stylistic sophistication, but in some ways it is a more fundamental and less forgivable naivety. It would, however, be ludicrous to argue that this represented some kind of failure on the part of modern science fiction to live up to its own paradigm. In fact, the reverse is true, for science fiction is more popular and more influential today than it has ever been. What my argument does imply is that the demand which science fiction meets, at least in today's world, may be *best* served—and very largely *is* served—by metaphysical fantasies.

VI.

THE MYTHOLOGY OF MAN-MADE CATASTROPHE

1. Introduction

All human life, everywhere, is haunted by the possibility of catastrophe. The degree of anxiety manifest in a particular society or felt by a particular individual may vary greatly, but there is no human situation which is free of it. A great deal of literary and dramatic art has, throughout history, been preoccupied with the possibilities of general or personal disaster. No culture lacks illustrations of disaster or prescriptions determining the appropriate attitudes and responses to disaster. Much imaginative endeavor has also gone into the attempt to provide reassurances that it is, after all, possible to avoid or survive catastrophe, if only we behave in an appropriate manner.

That this should be so is by no means surprising. Human existence depends on the ability to reason and the ability to foresee the possible future outcomes of the situations which confront us. If we could not anticipate disasters we could not avoid them, and it makes perfect pragmatic sense to be perpetually on the lookout for the possibility of disaster. When disaster threatens from without, we must be prepared to ward it off, or take evasive action—and we must, of course, be doubly cautious that our own actions do not precipitate disaster.

There is, however, no culture which is really objective in its attitudes to misfortune. All societies—and perhaps all individuals—sanction the belief that some people *deserve* to suffer, and that when catastrophe strikes the guilty the moral order of the universe is being conserved. Here, of course, human ideas about what ought to be the case frequently come into conflict with observations of what actually is the case, for (as St. Matthew and everyone else has observed) Heaven "sendeth rain on the just and on the unjust." The sense of satisfaction which we feel when the wicked are punished is bought at the price of a sense of confusion which we tend to feel when the innocent also suffer. We tend, in such cases, to seek special explanations—both history and cultural anthropology bear eloquent witness to the ingenuity which characteristically goes into the search. The scientific world-view which some members of modern Western culture have adopted is virtually unique in holding all such special explanations to be invalid, and holding fast to the logic of chance, which presumes that where natural catastrophes are concerned there is no earthly reason why the just should have any particular advantage over the unjust. Only where catastrophes are man-made does the scientific world-view leave room for a moral order. For this reason the characteristic attitudes displayed in science fiction stories about man-made catastrophes are markedly different from those displayed in stories of natural disaster.

Ours is perhaps the only culture where it is possible (because of the sacredness of the scientific world-view) for individuals and groups to suffer catastrophe without seeking to debit the moral responsibility for the misfortune from themselves or from others. It is *possible*—but it is not easy. The most-asked unanswerable question is still: "Why did it have to happen to *me*?"

The tribal societies which we are pleased to call "primitive" are never at a loss when called upon to preserve faith in the moral order of the universe in the face of disaster. For such societies, *all* catastrophes are man-made. If I fall ill, it is because the ancestral spirits have been angered by some failure of duty, or because I have broken a taboo. If I really am completely innocent of any such transgression, then witches are at work. Some tribesmen are more given to guilt than others—many societies allow witchcraft only as a rare and exceptional explanation, while others use it habitually.

The beliefs of the Azande, who find witchcraft everywhere, have been extracted from their context as an exemplary illustration of how unreasonable savages can be. *We* know that when a man sickens and dies he has been carried off by cancer or trypanosomes, and *we* know that the fact this man and no other was crossing the bridge when it collapsed is a coincidence of no significance. What we often fail to realize, however, is that we have paid a price for our entitlement to this intellectual snobbery. The pseudotheory of witchcraft functions in Azande society not so much as an explanation extending an understanding of the way the world works, but as an imaginative instrument which allows people confronted with misfortune to *do* something about it. It enables the tribesman to respond to catastrophe in a *meaningful* way, so that even in the absence of medical knowledge he can pit himself against the ravages of sickness, and need not feel helpless or that the universe has suffered a fall of moral parity. It is an awkward question for modern Western man to face when he asks himself who is better equipped—in purely pragmatic terms—to deal with the experience of grief and the horror of helplessness: the tribesman who hunts witches; the religious man who prays to God; or the rationalist who understands the workings of chance.

In the context of these observations we may, perhaps, be able to see one of the reasons why contemporary science fiction writers are so fascinated by disasters which come about not through the workings

THE MYTHOLOGY OF MAN-MADE CATASTROPHE

of blind cosmic chance but as a result of our own actions. There is a certain irony in the fact that science, which destroyed the moral order implicit in our traditional frames of reference, should also have given us the power to bring destruction upon ourselves on such a vast scale. The mythology of man-made catastrophe which we are in the process of building is replacing the taboos whose violation would once have angered our ancestors with a new set, whose violation will overpopulate and spoil the earth. The witches whose innate evil threatened the security of traditional communities are being replaced by different kinds of evil men, whose threat is certainly no less. The analysis of stories of man-made catastrophe will reveal them to be propaganda for new codes of social behavior, embodying new concepts of sin—or perhaps refurbishing old ones.

At first glance it appears that modern catastrophic fiction relies heavily for moral inspiration and implication on traditional catastrophist fantasy. There are few modern stories of flood or plague which do not refer back explicitly and metaphorically to the incidents in *Genesis* and *Exodus* when God instigated reprisals against human wickedness and Pharaonic intransigence. Closer inspection, however, will reveal that where we are dealing with writers whose allegiance is to the world-view of modern science rather than the presuppositions of religious doctrine the parallels are drawn specifically to be broken. Even in the works of twentieth-century writers whose commitment to Christianity is wholehearted we very often find an attitude to catastrophe which does not at all reflect the story of Noah. (An excellent example is provided by Alfred Noyes, author of the atomic holocaust story *The Last Man* and the holocaust-threat story *The Devil Takes a Holiday*. The latter story, in trying to come to terms with modern man's apparent predilection for self-destruction, breaks new theological ground in redefining the role of the devil.)

It is not too difficult to find stories which provide crucial turning points in the imaginative attribution of significance to catastrophe. In John Beresford's "A Negligible Experiment," the impending doom of the Earth is taken (by a scientist) to imply not that God has tired of human wickedness once and for all, but that God has grown tired of a trivial experiment and is moving on to new fields. In such a scheme there is no room for Noah and the Ark. The personal catastrophe which strikes down the hero of H. G. Wells's *The Undying Fire* becomes an exemplary visitation developed in parallel with the story of Job. The moral of the tale is in one way similar: what is called for is a massive reinforcement of faith. In another way, though, it is also crucially different—in the important matter of what the new Job is required to believe *in*. Later in his career, Wells was also to recast the story of Noah to hold a related moral: the hero of *All Aboard for Ararat* accepts his commission only on condition that God steps down from his exalted position to allow man (aided by science) to adopt the crucial role of moral guide and guardian.

The tendency for modern practitioners of exemplary catastrophism to borrow metaphors from older traditions has been greatly encouraged by the fact that our cultural heritage is particularly rich in imaginative strategies for dealing with the question of moral responsibility for misfortune. The scapegoat strategy of the Azande is amply represented in the history of Medieval Christendom by the slaughter of the Jews in the wake of the Black Death and by the witch-craze which attended the decay of the Roman Catholic Empire of Faith, and has also been echoed in more recent times. The notion of divine retribution occasioned by the breaking of taboos is amply represented by that fraction of our religious imagination which derives from the Old Testament. In addition to these strategies we also have (again courtesy of the Old Testament) the story of Job, which cunningly suggests that the misfortunes of the innocent might be a test of their faith. This notion is particuarly ingenious in that it removes altogether the notion of *guilt*, and it may perhaps be something of a tragedy that the Christian world much preferred its own imaginative *tour de force*, the concept of original sin, which abolished instead the notion of innocence. This unusual versatility of the Western religious imagination permits catastrophists to draw morals from their stories in several different ways, and not all of them are out of keeping with a rationalistic world-view. The Darwinian theory of natural selection has (for social Darwinists, at least) put a new gloss on the notion of the catastrophe-as-test; while the science of genetics, especially when its implications are misconstrued, has allowed new meaning to be injected into the notion of original sin.

Another thing to remember when we find modern tales of disaster drawing metaphors from the literature of the ancient world is that ours is not the first Western culture to have coped with the rise of rationalism. The Greeks invented science, and *their* exemplary literature quite frequently exposes genuine parallels with our own style of thought, with the one important difference that we have taken rationalism and science somewhat further than they. *We* live in a *post*-Promethean age.

The scientific imagination, in providing a new mythology of catastrophe, has to overturn the old mythologies provided by the religious imagination, but it has no option but to reflect them even as it transfigures them. In so doing it is subject to a curious restraint, in that much of the vocabulary we have built up in order to talk about possible catastrophes is derived directly from particular religious myths. The words, in consequence, cannot help but carry implications which are antipathetic to the new meanings which the scientific imagination wishes to impose upon them. The words which we use to talk about the possibility of impending doom are colored with echoes of religious mythology, and none more so than the word *apocalypse*, which carries

THE MYTHOLOGY OF MAN-MADE CATASTROPHE

with it a whole host of imagistic associations. From the same source, of course, we acquire *Armageddon* and the *Millennium*. The very use of the words confers ambiguity upon modern fantasies in which they feature strongly, and they recall metaphors whose mesmeric power is obvious even when they are used ironically (as, for instance, in Norman Spinrad's story, "The Big Flash"). The main consequence of this fact is that we can see in twentieth-century catastrophist fiction a curious kind of ideative resonance, by which the apparatus of the religious imagination echoes in the literature of the scientific imagination as a series of apparitions. Look, if you will, at the illustrations in the pulp magazine *Famous Fantastic Mysteries*, which was for a long time filled with stories of the end of the world, and see how frequently religious symbolism is employed to capture the mood of such stories.

In the discussion of literary works which follows, I shall make abundant use of such loaded words as "apocalypse" and "Armageddon." I shall also refer back frequently to ancient myths whose function was to allocate moral responsibility and to define different kinds of misconduct. This should not be allowed to distract attention from the fact that what is really under scrutiny is the construction of a *new* mythology of moral responsibility, and we are concerned not with the reaffirmation but with the metamorphosis of our concepts of sin.

2. *The Advent of the Age of Anxiety*

It might be argued that what it has become fashionable to call "the Age of Anxiety" began when people realized that they were not, in fact, responsible for catastrophe, and that an entirely arbitrary disaster (a plague or a cometary collision) might wipe out mankind at any time. The rationalists of the Enlightenment could stop worrying that God might send another deluge to punish their apostasy, but they also had to stop believing in a divine protective power that would make sure nothing happened to the chosen people. The Age of Anxiety in this view would be correlated in its rise with a developing awareness of man's vulnerability to *natural* catastrophe.

If we follow this line of argument, however, we are constrained to point out that there arose in the wake of this feeling of apprehension a different sense of threat which redoubled our sense of existential insecurity, for the rediscovery of the possibility of *man-made* catastrophe created a feeling rather different from the one men had when all misfortunes were punishments or sorceries. The new mythology of man-made catastrophe—the essentially *science-fictional* mythology—stressed that the mundane activities of ordinary human beings might set in train sequences of cause-and-effect which could destroy civilization. This was a new idea. It surfaced less than a hundred years ago, and perhaps correlates better with the application of the label,

"Age of Anxiety." Being at the mercy of Nature caused us only mild concern; being at one another's mercy was quite another matter.

There are actually very few nineteenth-century stories which invite description as tales of man-made catastrophe, though there is a certain touch of foreboding in many stories of personal tragedy. It is not too difficult today to read Mary Shelley's *Frankenstein* (1818) as a kind of parable in which the unlucky scientist represents modern man in his totality, threatened with destruction at the hands of the monsters of his own creation. This interpretation certainly helped Brian W. Aldiss to find in *Frankenstein* not only the first but also the *archetypal* science fiction novel, but its force would not have been appreciated by Mary Shelley. The same is true of some other mid-century parables, including Herman Melville's Renaissance fantasy, "The Bell-Tower," which has been annexed by some recent science fiction historians. The theme does appear once in nineteenth-century imaginative fiction, in the section of Samuel Butler's *Erewhon* (1872) which is entitled "The Book of the Machines," but there it is only the ghost of an idea; Butler refrains from lending wholehearted endorsement to the Erewhonians' reasons for abandoning machinery. Butler had first put forward the idea that man might be overtaken and enslaved by his machines in the article, "Darwin Among the Machines" (1863), which he signed "Cellarius," but he replied to his own article with an opposing argument in 1865, his tone throughout being ironic. "The Book of the Machines" anticipates an important twentieth-century argument, but the anticipation does not really testify to considerable foresight on Butler's part. A much more realistic—and certainly sincere—fear of the effect machines might have on human life was that expressed in William Morris's *News from Nowhere* (1891), which is by no means a Catastrophist work.

In fact, of course, nineteenth-century attitudes to technology were overwhelmingly optimistic. The fruits of the steam engine were welcomed far and wide; it represented in the eyes of most visionaries a way to free men from drudgery and to increase the productive capacity of society so much that every man might become wealthy. There were plenty of people who observed the unpleasant consequences of industrialization, who abhorred the growth of filthy cities and the creation of the new urban poor; but they were far more ready to blame poor social institutions for this kind of misery than the machines themselves. We see in nineteenth-century English literature many eloquent pleas for political reform, but hardly any sympathy for the Luddites. The one striking exception is Richard Jefferies's *After London* (1885), which looks forward to the day when the ruins of the great cities are no more than poisonous sores in a rural landscape. Though the reversion to barbarism of England's populace is described in the first part of the novel, the nature of the catastrophe is deliberately unspecified, and is perhaps to be regarded as the working of an ironic Fate rather than either a natural or man-made disaster.

THE MYTHOLOGY OF MAN-MADE CATASTROPHE

Most nineteenth-century writers concerned with anticipating future technological developments regarded the industrial revolution as a prelude to Utopia. The archetypal expression of this view was Edward Bellamy's best-selling novel, *Looking Backward* (1888). There were plenty of objectors to Bellamy's view of the socialist Utopia, including William Morris, but most of the replies to his novel are alternative Utopias, few of which dispute the necessity or desirability of mechanization. The one major catastrophist reply—Ignatius Donnelly's *Caesar's Column*—objects only to Bellamy's premise regarding the direction of socioeconomic "evolution." Technology provides Donnelly's world-destroyers with the means, but the *cause* of the holocaust is the nature of the Capitalist system.

In *Caesar's Column* the catastrophe is twice man-made: it is revolution led by the "Brotherhood of Destruction," but made necessary by the greed of the capitalists who control the world's wealthy and keep the working class in conditions of grinding poverty. Donnelly's assumptions differ very little from those of Marx, but what sets him apart from most quasi-Marxist socialists is precisely his catastrophism: most Marxists looked forward to the revolution as a means of liberation. Marx did, of course, anticipate that the revolution might be bloody, but he did not consider that this blood was on anyone's hands—according to his economic thesis the revolution was inevitable, and the role of Marxists was to lessen the birth-pangs of the new world by acting as "midwives." In the view of orthodox Marxists, the catastrophic aspects of the revolution were to be classed as a *natural* disaster—only its positive aspects were to be regarded as man-made. Donnelly dissented from this, believing that the revolution could and should be avoided if only men would commit themselves to Christian values in their economic transactions.

Not everyone, of course, saw revolution in the same way. For Marx, it was both inevitable and desirable, so that it was neither man-made nor a catastrophe. For Donnelly, it was clearly undesirable, but was only inevitable if men declined to act. For others—especially those who felt threatened by the possibility of a rebellion of the lower classes—there was no doubt at all that revolution constituted a man-made catastrophe; and it is in connection with such political anxieties that we can identify nineteenth-century imaginative fictions which most nearly approach the subject matter of this essay. The exploits of the Revolutionary Tribunal in Paris in 1793 created anxiety in Britain, and the history of the ill-fated Paris Commune of 1871 seemed to provide a further moral lesson. Accounts of such imaginary uprisings were, however, limited by the presumption that no really effective destructive power would be available to the revolutionaries. Anarchists armed with airships did not appear until 1893, when E. Douglas Fawcett produced *Hartmann the Anarchist; or, The Doom of the Great City*. The scale of violence in that book is not quite parochial, but it is hardly apocalyptic.

Destruction on a far vaster scale was featured in another novel of Terrorist uprising published the same year—George Griffith's *The Angel of the Revolution*—but here the Terrorists are the heroes and the world is being liberated rather than raped.

The prospect of a socialist revolution, however, was not the most important cause for political concern in late nineteenth-century Britain. Much more attention was paid to the possibility of international war, and it was this prospect which exercised the most powerful influence over futuristic fiction. From 1871, when Chesney published his imaginary account of "The Battle of Dorking" as a piece of propaganda for rearmament, until 1914, when the Great War at last broke out, war-anticipation stories were the most prolific species of futuristic fiction in Europe.

It would be a mistake to consider all the future war stories of this period as Catastrophist fictions. The prospect of *losing* a war was, of course, a prospect which no one could tolerate, but the prospect of a successful war was something else. To many of the writers who participated in the debate aroused by Chesney's fictional essay, war was still a great adventure, to be commenced for the sheer fun of it but by no means to be shirked. There are many British stories of possible invasion which recognize the truly disastrous nature of that prospect, but the authors almost invariably relished the opportunity which such scenarios offered for tales of heroism and glorious derring-do. There were very few writers who displayed the least trace of the attitude which became commonplace in the future war stories written *after* the Great War: the view that involvement in war is a catastrophe for *everyone*, winners and losers alike.

Before 1914, war could still be regarded as a game, especially by those whose attitudes had been fixed by a knowledge of history. The horrors of war had been made known to the British by reportage of war in the Crimea in 1854-56, but this was a war fought on foreign soil, in which only soldiers were involved (on the British side, at least). The weapons used there were extremely limited in their destructive capabilities. It was this kind of contest which was imaginatively associated with the notion of a future war by the majority of nineteenth-century writers. Only a very small number of men realized the extent to which technology could and must remake war. Some of these were among the European observers in the American Civil War, who had seen glimpses of the future in the use of breech-loading rifled guns, machine-guns, ironclad ships, observation balloons, flame-throwers, poison gas, and submarines. Few of these things had made any significant impact on the actual fighting, but their existence was sufficient to create an awareness of threat in the minds of those with sufficient imagination. This awareness grew steadily through the half century which separated the end of the Civil War from the beginning of the Great War, but before 1900 there were really only three writers of futuristic romance who foresaw the possible nature of a new war. These three were George Griffith, author of *The Angel of the Revolution*; M. P. Shiel, author of *The Yellow Danger* (1898); and H. G. Wells, author of *When the Sleeper Wakes* (1899). None of these novels, however, can be regarded as Catastrophist fantasies. *When the Sleeper Wakes* is, like The *Angel of the Revolution*, a story of a liberating revolution whose inevitability has been assured by socioeconomic factors. *The Yellow Danger*, which involves the annihilation of the entire populations of Asia and the European mainland by means of bacterial warfare, excuses its excesses by means of the logic of social Darwinism. Of the three, only Wells went on to cultivate an attitude to war which was much more in keeping with the wholehearted Catastrophist view that became commonplace in the 1920s.

One striking aspect of the war-anticipation stories of the nineteenth century, including those cited above, is the dominance of the notion of a "war to end war." Those writers who did foresee death and destruction on a vast scale believed to a man that such horrors could be justified as the necessary prelude to a new way of life. The greater the wars envisaged by these stories, the stronger was the commitment to the notion that they would represent a final settlement of all accounts. This combination of ideas helps to explain the essential moral ambiguity of the attitude to war manifest in these stories. No one before 1900 used speculative fiction in order to stigmatize the impulse to make war as a species of original sin.

The notion of using new and extremely powerful weapons to put an end to war forever was one which cropped up regularly in nineteenth-century imaginative fiction, when the logic of ultimate deterrents seems to have been very widely accepted. Examples include *The Vril Staff* (1891) by "X.Y.Z." and *His Wisdom, the Defender* (1900) by Simon Newcomb, where single individuals put crucial inventions into the hands of a benevolent few. Many future war novels gave a crucial role in deciding the course of such conflicts to inventions made by lone scientific geniuses. There was, however, an unpleasant corollary to this line of thought. If lone inventors could discover weapons so dreadful that they might terrify the world into peace, what of such inventions in the wrong hands? It is in connection with this notion that we discover the few wholeheartedly Catastrophist stories of the nineteenth century which focus directly on *man-made* catastrophes. They are fantasies of evil scientists—frequently mad scientists—who threaten the world with destruction. An early example is *The Crack of Doom* (1895) by Robert Cromie. In virtually all stories of this type, the would-be world-wreckers are thwarted, but the plot nevertheless shows a developing awareness of the *vulnerability* of society to the destructive power of new inventions.

The principal limitation placed on both the future war story and the mad scientist story was, of course, the kind of weapons which the contending forces could be imagined to possess. The main reason why the stories of these kinds produced in the last years of the nineteenth century differ so markedly from those produced even in the early years of the twentieth century is that in the space of a few years, from 1895 to 1898, a great deal of new imaginative fuel was added to speculation about future weaponry by certain unexpected discoveries in science. Before 1895 it was easy enough to imagine battles fought by airships and submarines, but these were primarily important in modifying the way that battles might be fought rather than adding to the destructive power of the opposing armies. That submarines might make sea travel extremely dangerous, and that the advent of the aeroplane would make the aerial bombing of cities possible, were realized by some writers—notably Griffith—but even these possibilities seemed inadequate as a recipe for Armageddon.

In 1895, though, Röntgen discovered X-rays and Becquerel described the property of "radioactivity" in uranium. Both discoveries were widely publicized, and the following year saw publication by Marconi of his work on wireless telegraphy. So dawned, in the popular imagination, the age of miraculous rays and no-longer-unsplittable atoms. These discoveries provided an imaginative *carte-blanche* for technological fantasies of all kinds, including stories involving weapons of miraculous potency. It was the notions of death-rays and disintegrator-rays which fed the new apocalyptic imagination, together with the less popular but more prophetic notion of atomic bombs. By 1900 it was a great deal easier to imagine that the power to annihilate mankind might one day rest in human hands than it had been in 1894; and it was this expansion of imaginative power which made the year 1900 a genuine *fin de siècle*. The discoveries of Röntgen and Becquerel gave speculative fiction the imaginative ammunition needed to take technological fantasies far beyond the boundaries which had previously confined them, to perceive many new wonders, and to see for the first time those unfortunate possibilities which lurked just beyond the imaginative horizon.

3. The Lotus Eaters

In 1930 Geoffrey Dennis published a painstaking study of the apocalyptic mythology of modern science, *The End of the World*. The book discusses the various possible ends of the earth revealed by contemporary knowledge, and considers the relative likelihood of each one. It considers also the possibility that man might become extinct before the death of the earth, and the possibility that men might actually outlive their home world by migrating to others. Concerning man's possible contribution to the end of the world, however, Dennis has little to say. The possibility of a war so destructive as to wipe out the race is

THE MYTHOLOGY OF MAN-MADE CATASTROPHE

not even mentioned *en passant* (though it figures large, for obvious reasons, in Kenneth Heuer's identically-titled study published in 1953). There is, however, one possible route to human extinction that he does consider in detail, and that is the notion that man might doom himself to extinction by choosing a way of life that leads the species to gradual degeneration. Indeed, he summarizes—though he is reluctant to endorse it—a common contemporary argument to the effect that this is already happening:

> Civilization is sapping man's vigour, blunting his senses, always reducing the scope for his endeavour. He no longer needs strong right arm nor mental resource, no longer need fend for himself, the super-State is his protector, his poisoner, according him cheap survival for an ever smaller expenditure of brain and brawn. State and faculty have joined their murderous hands. Medicine, while saving the individual, enfeebles the race; the proportion of weaklings is mounting like a tide of death....Tools do our "manual" work for us; the hand is losing its cunning, and with it a rich area of the brain its cunning also. When tools for mental work soon appear, the brain's brightest regions will follow little toe and little finger into atrophy.[1]

Dennis was by no means alone in regarding this process of degeneration as the chief threat facing human life. The magazine *Today and Tomorrow* published in its first issue (October 1930) an article by C. E. M. Joad called "Is Civilization Doomed?" in which the author advanced a similar argument. Joad, too, is reluctant to endorse it as a true vision of the future, stating that he considers it his duty to be as pessimistic as possible in the hope of alerting his fellow men to the dangers which face them in time for them to take the appropriate action.

This kind of attitude takes its inspiration from the Darwinian theory of evolution, and in particular from the notion of "the survival of the fittest" in "the struggle for existence." If this were the key to evolutionary ascendancy, it could easily be argued that, by exempting himself from the struggle for existence man might suffer a drastic loss of biological "fitness." In point of fact, the argument is based on a misunderstanding of the nature of genetic inheritance, but it retained its influence in the popular imagination long after the rediscovery of Mendelian theory. The line of argument is particularly obvious in early Wells—in the portrayal of the society of the Eloi in *The Time Machine* (1895), and in the careful attempt to preserve the biological fitness of the Samurai, masters of the new world in *A Modern Utopia* (1905). It was, of course, an argument very effectively deployed against technological Utopianism by E. M. Forster in "The Machine Stops" (1909).

Forster's version of the case is particularly strong in that it avoids the use of spurious pseudo-biology. He simply imagines a society where all needs are mechanically supplied, and where people in consequence have become idle, impotent, and depersonalized. They have neither the knowledge nor the spirit necessary to cope with the disaster that follows the failure of their machines. Other writers were prepared to suggest that such a dispirited society might not need the *coup de grâce* of disaster: James Elroy Flecker's story of "The Last Generation" (1908) is an account of the mass resignation of the human race from the business of living, which has come to seem rather pointless. A much more elaborate explication of the same idea was provided by S. Fowler Wright a generation later in *The Adventure of Wyndham Smith* (1938). The sentiments expressed in these stories are genuinely anti-Utopian, arguing that if society should ever reach the point where all men can live in harmony, with all their desires gratified without effort, then life itself becomes literally purposeless.

In his book on *The English Utopia* (1952), A. L. Morton points out that Utopian speculation, though it may represent the social aspirations of different classes and different individuals in particular sets of historical circumstances, is rooted in a fundamental "image of desire" which he terms "the Utopia of the folk." His archetypal example is the fourteenth-century poem, *The Land of Cokaygne*, which describes "an earthly and earthy paradise, an island of magical abundance, of eternal youth and eternal summer, of joy, fellowship and peace." It is a land where no one has to do any work, where everything is free, and where there are no duties of religious observance. The last point is of cardinal importance, for the poem is an anti-clerical satire as well as a wish-fulfillment dream, and it serves to remind us that this Utopia of the folk stood to be condemned as depraved, immoral, and degenerate. The notion that a life of ease and comfort is both extremely attractive and utterly reprehensible is much older than the myth of Cokaygne: it is embodied in the myth of the lotus-eaters who were briefly visited by Odysseus and whose way of life was recorded by Herodotus and Pliny. In this form, and in the fourteenth-century poem, it is a myth of a miraculous ecology, but in its twentieth-century version it becomes a myth of miraculous technology.

The alternate world of Cokaygne becomes a technological reality in "The City of the Living Dead" (1930) by Laurence Manning and Fletcher Pratt, in which most of the inhabitants of Earth's cities elect to have their sensory organs removed and replaced with wires piping synthetic experience directly into their brains. The cities die as everyone retreats to live in his dreams. The people are helpless before the possibility of a malfunction, but it is not so much the prospect of their dying which is represented horrifically as their predicament in life;

THE MYTHOLOGY OF MAN-MADE CATASTROPHE

in particular, the way that they have blinded themselves in order to control exactly what they may see.

The condemnation of the city dwellers in this story (which is offered, in fact, by one of their number) has two principal components. On the one hand, the wonderful lives which they lead are not *real*, and the acceptance of ersatz experience is seen to be a kind of moral failure. On the other hand, the universality of the practice has led society into a blind alley—it has put an end to progress. This double indictment recurs frequently in stories published during the last half-century, particularly those concerned with the invention of new media of communication. When James Olds discovered that direct stimulation of a particular area in the hind-brain of a rat had an effect so powerful that a rat given the means to self-stimulation would repeat the appropriate action until it dropped from exhaustion, tolerating no distractions, the implications fit readily enough into our suspicions about human psychology.

The most comprehensive science-fictional account of the fate of a society equipped with the technological means to take the philosophy of hedonism to its logical extreme is to be found in James E. Gunn's *The Joy Makers* (1961). The last part of the story—originally published as "The Naked Sky" in 1955—features a more sophisticated version of the same imagery that was displayed in "City of the Living Dead." In Mack Reynolds's *After Utopia* (1977) a high-technology society which has solved all the social problems of today faces the spread of "dream machines" which threaten the same eventuality. A political radical brought forward out of our own time is given the problem of saving the world from stagnation, and accepts it willingly, inventing an external threat which convinces the people that they cannot yet retreat into themselves secure in the knowledge that they will be left in peace. (The solution seems, at best, to be temporary.)

The value judgments expressed in these stories are taken so completely for granted that the moral philosophy behind them rarely becomes wholly explicit. It is not too difficult to see what the clergy of the fourteenth century had against the land of Cokaygne. In their view, men did have duties of religious observance which they must not shirk, and the means of production available to the society of the day were such that it could support very few idlers. Neither of these arguments can be held to apply to the futuristic states imagined in these modern stories. Though condemnation is no less strong, the nature of the moral complaints has altered.

The fact that a preference for ersatz experience over real is seen as a moral failure has much to do with a conviction that lies at the heart of the rationalistic scientific world-view: that subjective experiences are worthless by comparison with "public" experience of the external world. This judgment is, of course, crucial to the ascent of empiricism to its privileged position in modern philosophy, and to its total dominance of the philosophy of knowledge. The worthlessness of experience which is private and cannot be corroborated by objective evidence is central to the contemporary philosophy of science. The advancement of this claim is held to provide the foundation stone of a value-free science, but this should not obscure the fact that the claim itself is a value judgment. It implies that dalliance with subjective experience is a kind of self-betrayal, a wicked preference for ignorance and illusion over the true path of enlightenment. It is this line of argument which has made the term "escapism" into an inherently pejorative one. (There is a certain irony in the fact that imaginative fiction, which is frequently charged with being pure escapism, frequently adopts a moral stance which is harshly critical of escapism.)

Positivism—the most radical form of empiricism—has declined in popularity in the last few decades, partly because of new fashions in the philosophy of the social sciences and because of the exploits of sociologists of knowledge, who have exposed allegedly fraudulent aspects of the orthodox representation of scientific method. It might be expected that this will soon be reflected in science fiction by the appearance of apologists who will defend the city of the living dead against the well-meaning Luddites, but to date there is not much sign of this. It is, however, noticeable that a more tolerant attitude occasionally crops up. In the *Star Trek* episode "The Menagerie," the crippled starship captain Christopher Pike, totally helpless in the real world, is allowed to retreat (along with his aged and enfeebled female companion) into a world of pleasant illusion, taking with him the good wishes of the entire *dramatis personae*. Perhaps more significantly, the concluding volume of Michael Moorcock's "Dancers at the End of Time" trilogy, *The End of All Songs* (1976), allows the decadent immortals to continue their theatrical existence in a bubble of eternity sealed against the ravages of entropy, while a few of their number set off to create the universe anew. The creative few still have the moral advantage, but there is a sympathy for the lotus eaters which finds no echo in *The Joy Makers*.

The second charge levelled at lotus eater societies—that they have forsaken progress—is perhaps easier to understand. The advance of technology, in the popular imagination, *is* progress, and the notion that it should someday lead to the death of progress almost smacks of paradox. The worthiness of progress has been doubted far more widely than the unworthiness of subjective experience, but this doubt has affected the science fiction community less than most, and in science fiction progress is often elevated to the status of the greatest good. In Mack Reynolds's "United Planets" series the sole criterion for the evaluation of a political system is whether or not it permits progress (*i.e.*, innovation and the growth of scientific understanding). The growth of anti-technological movements in society has sometimes been subject to scathing criticism in science fiction—a good example is the examination of near-future prospects presented in "Spirals" (1979) by Larry Niven and Jerry Pournelle. One of the reasons why science fiction writers are so prolific in their presentation of primitive societies (whether post-holocaust cultures or colonies on other worlds) is that it is easy enough in the context of such societies to see *what counts* as progress, and therefore what goals each society has. Considering the nature of the genre, it is astonishing how shy contemporary science fiction writers are of imagining societies in which the problems of the present-day world have been adequately solved. Again, as the myth of progress declines in the real world, we may begin to see science fiction stories presenting apologies for non-progressive worlds; but what seems more likely to happen is that our definitions of progress will change. In its original meaning, the word "progress" had little to do with technology and much to do with the notion of moral perfectibility, and science fiction already gives evidence of the return swing of the pendulum in the prolific postwar mythology of future human evolution.

In the light of this characteristic emphasis on progress it is ironic that most stories criticizing lotus eater societies can find no solution to the problem except smashing the machines and starting all over again. The irony is revealed for appreciation in Isaac Asimov's "The Life and Times of Multivac" (1975), which takes a fresh look at the question of what happens when the machine stops.

The fact that there is no such solution to be found demonstrates the real heart of the problem, which is a lack of faith in ourselves. The whole issue would seem quite unproblematic if we were not so ready to see in ourselves this predilection for degeneracy. We tend to see the society of the technologically-assisted lotus eaters as a "no win" situation: in itself it constitutes a catastrophe of one kind, whereas the way out of the predicament involves a catastrophic return to primitive circumstances. We see no other alternatives because the ideative seed from which these images grow is so deeply implanted; it is the notion that human beings are, in their fundamental psychological nature, fatally flawed. No one believes that a significant fraction of the human race could actually withstand the temptation of the dream machines; we conceive of ourselves as being helpless in the face of addiction to pleasure-seeking. It is, of course, highly significant that we chose to label the addictive circuit in the brain discovered by Olds "the pleasure center."

It is this notion of basic flaws in human nature which lies at the heart of the mythology of man-made catastrophe. We no longer think of these supposed flaws as "original sin," except in metaphor, but their role has not changed. Science fiction writers, in particular, conceive of them as the legacy of our evolutionary biology: primitive "drives" and "urges" which, for all our piety and wit, we cannot overcome, the moving finger of evolution having written indelibly upon our being. The notion has been bandied about abundantly in recent popular science and pseudoscience, notably in the works of Robert Ardrey and

Desmond Morris, and perhaps most dramatically in Carl Sagan's exposition of the myth of the triple-brain, *The Dragons of Eden*.

The myth of the dream machine—of the technologically-supported society of lotus eaters—is only one facet of this image of flawed humanity. Several others exist, and all are associated with particular traditions of catastrophist fiction. All of them are interlinked, but some of them are in conflict, and come to the verge of contradicting one another. Before we pass on, however, to look at some of the other fatal flaws which are popularly considered to mar human nature, it is necessary to point out one particular variant of the myth of the lotus eaters notable for the extremism of its imagery. This is the line of thought which develops from Butler's "Book of the Machines," and which construes "degeneracy" not in a moral sense but in a physical sense as well.

Butler, commenting on the Erewhonian treatise on machines, offers the following summary of the case:

> The one serious danger which this writer apprehended was that the machines would so equalize men's powers, and so lessen the severity of competition, that many persons of inferior physique would escape detection and transmit their inferiority to their descendants. He feared that the removal of the present pressure might cause a degeneracy of the human race, and indeed that the whole body might become rudimentary, the man himself being nothing but soul and mechanism, an intelligent but passionless principle of mechanical action.[2]

Wells, of course, was to follow an identical line of argument in developing his image of "The Man of the Year Million"—a creature with a massive head and withered body, incapable even of supporting himself. We find this image repeated in many early pulp science fiction stories, most notably in "Twilight" (1934) and "Night" (1935) by John W. Campbell Jr. writing as "Don A. Stuart," and in "Alas, All Thinking!" (1935) by Harry Bates. Several early stories by David H. Keller, including "The Revolt of the Pedestrians" and "Stenographers' Hands" (both 1928) feature more specific accounts of physical degeneration occasioned by unnatural selection.

The most significant thing about *this* line of argument (as opposed to that followed by "City of the Living Dead," *The Joy Makers*, etc.) is that it is entirely false, having its basis in a pseudo-Lamarckian notion of inheritance. The fact that unused muscles will atrophy and become useless is irrelevant to any consideration of genetic deterioration, in that acquired characteristics are not transmitted from one generation to the next. It may be true that civilization—and modern medicine in particular—preserves within the gene pool certain genotypes which would otherwise be eliminated, but such an increase in the "genetic load" carried by a species does not set in train a degenerative process affecting all the individuals within the population. Even though the selection operating against deleterious genes is muted in its effects, it will still work in favor of more favorable genes, and certainly not in such a way as to exclude them from the gene pool, however gradually.

Fictions such as "Twilight," in fact, are not extrapolative fictions at all, and have much more in common with the Victorian myths concerning the effects of masturbation: they represent an urgent call for moral rearmament, whose propagandistic priorities override the question of fidelity to empirical realism. Their plea is that we should not, and must not, relax and be satisfied, and their fear is that a representation of the actual effects of succumbing to the fruits of the technological lotus is an insufficient deterrent. The fundamental assumption of this line of argument is that the temptation is virtually irresistible, and they are very probably right.

4. *Epimetheus Unbound*

The fear that machines might make us all too comfortable is, of course, by no means the only anxiety which we feel concerning the advance of technology. Indeed, the danger that we all might retreat into private worlds of synthetic experience exists in parallel with the suspicion that our developing technology might ultimately destroy the very possibility of private experience. If machines have the power to give us all perfect freedom (albeit within the limits of an artificial solipsism), then they also have the power to take away our freedom altogether—to make us subject to manipulation and oppression and the most absolute of tyrannies.

There are two versions of this mythology. In the first, the development of new techology gives the ruling elite within society the power to perpetuate its rule indefinitely, and to refine progressively the extent of its command over the lives and thoughts of the underdogs. All the most striking images in twentieth-century dystopian fiction derive from this line of thought: the watchful mechanical eyes of *Nineteen Eighty-Four*, the entire apparatus of social control in Huxley's *Brave New World*, etc. In the second version the power elite have become redundant, and the machines themselves are the manipulators and oppressors, and sometimes the destroyers of humankind.

Like the story of the physical degeneration of the species, the story of the revolt of the machines is primarily of figurative significance. Many such stories make no pretence of realism, and invite a straightforward allegorical reading: Robert Bloch's "It Happened Tomorrow" (1943), Clifford D. Simak's "Bathe Your Bearings in Blood" (also known as "Skirmish," 1950), and Lord Dunsany's *The Last Rev-*

olution (1950) are typical examples. There are, however, versions of the myth which are better rationalized, and since the second world war we have made such vast strides in the development of machine intelligence that a good many fantasies of the prewar period have been re-endorsed with frightening plausibility.

The anxiety, in its simplest form, has been dubbed by Isaac Asimov "the Frankenstein Syndrome," and it is displayed with particular moral clarity in Karel Capek's work, particularly the play, *R.U.R.* (1921). In this story the "robots" produced by man to do his work for him eventually become so perfectly adapted to the task that they replace him altogether, going to war to remove him once he has made himself quite redundant. In another of his works, the novel *The Absolute at Large* (1922), Capek describes a worldwide catastrophe precipitated by the development of an atomic engine, the *karburator,* which annihilates matter and releases the spirit bound up within it—a spirit with which man is ill-equipped to cope.

These stories represent the inventor not as Prometheus (a common nineteenth-metaphor), but as Epimetheus, unwisely accepting "gifts" from his gods, with the consequence that his curiosity releases a plague of troubles upon mankind.

Parables following this line of thought ask not "what happens when the machine stops?" or "what will happen to us if it works as intended?" but "what happens when the machine malfunctions, or when our discoveries turn out to have unfortunate corollaries?" Mechanical brains in science fiction show a distinct tendency to go mad, or to have no sense of social responsibility in carrying out their instructions. While science-fictional machines quite frequently defy such trivial constraints as the law of conservation of energy, they hardly ever defy Sod's Law—the principle that if something can go wrong, it will.

Hugo Gernsback founded *Amazing Stories* in order to inspire young readers with magnificent dreams of the wonderful future that science would create. He himself was a Utopian optimist of indomitable naivety, but the great majority of the stories which were written for his magazines actually featured technology gone wrong: the marvellous machines fell more frequently into the wrong hands than the right ones, and very often they were troublesome entirely on their own account. The world was almost invariably saved, but the significant thing is the fact that it was constantly in need of saving. A particularly eloquent early example of mechanization-anxiety of this kind is Miles J. Breuer's *Paradise and Iron* (1930), in which the inhabitants of a Utopian island find themselves suddenly under threat when the artificial brain co-ordinating its advanced domestic and agricultural machinery begins to malfunction. Similar plots have remained a part of the staple diet of magazine science fiction, more modern variants being Philip K. Dick's "Autofac" (1955) and John Sladek's *The Reproductive System* (also known as *Mechasm*, 1968). In contemporary science fiction computers

THE MYTHOLOGY OF MAN-MADE CATASTROPHE

frequently aspire not only to emulate man but even to emulate God. Asimov, the arch-apologist for technology in general and artificial intelligence in particular, wrote numerous stories in which the usurpation of human privileges by robots is seen as being by no means catastrophic; and in "The Last Question" (1956) he is quite sympathetic to the Godly ambitions of a computer. Other writers, however, have taken a rather darker view of these prospects—examples include Philip K. Dick's *Vulcan's Hammer* (1960), *Larger than Life* (1960) by Dino Buzzati, *Colossus* (1966) and its sequels by D. F. Jones, and the surreal "I Have No Mouth and I Must Scream" (1967) by Harlan Ellison. The computer's view of the situation is amply represented by the satirical moral fable, *The Tale of the Big Computer* (also known as *The Great Computer*, 1966) by the Nobel prize-winning author, Hannes Álfvén, writing as "Olaf Johannesson."

An important aspect of this kind of story is that very often the artificial intelligences involved are not malicious. Sometimes they go mad because they are "too human"—as in several ridiculous stories in which robots or computers fall in love with their creators and subsequently suffer awful frustration and jealousy—but more often they cause trouble simply by trying to do their best. Machines which are too helpful are featured in several stories, including Murray Leinster's "A Logic Named Joe" (1946) and Jack Williamson's classic "With Folded Hands" (1947). Those stories which describe the logic by which computers come to consider themselves superior to man normally concede that there is some justification in the decision, and that the machines have an adequate warrant for their belief.

As time has gone by we have become more and more concerned about the *side effects* of technology—the unintended consequences of discovery. Industrial waste has been with us for a long time, but it is only recently that we have begun to fear that the negative effects of industry upon the environment may outweigh the positive effects of its products on the quality of our lives. In recent years, too, we have become much more sensitive to the prospect of a major accident involving some product of our technology—the escape of a new bacillus or an explosion at a nuclear power station. Catastrophist fantasies associated with these anxieties generally promote the allegation that we are downright irresponsible, and will be discussed further in a later section of this essay; but the indictment levelled by stories of the revolt of the machines and technological oppression are not primarily criticisms of human irresponsibility. Rather, they serve to put the argument that knowledge and wisdom are not identical, and that we have far more of the former than the latter.

Curiosity, it is said, kills the cat, and this proverb extends its implications into imaginative fiction in two ways. First, there is the story whose moral is that "there are things man was not meant to know"—stories where the truth is awful and enlightenment almost always fatal. Archetypal examples are the horror fantasies of H. P. Lovecraft. Science fiction has little room for this kind of story, which is implicitly anti-scientific. There is also, however, the story whose moral is that in matters of scientific discovery one has to take the rough with the smooth—there is no guarantee that the technological possibilities revealed by the advancement of science will necessarily be edifying. This is a lesson that we have learned well enough by courtesy of the atom bomb.

Stories of disasters which come about because of new inventions usually stress that the real root cause of the disaster is the element in human nature which drives us to seek advantage over our fellow men. In stories of technological oppression the men who already have those advantages are given greater power to indulge them and greater power to secure them. In stories where machines take over the world, they are merely reflecting (often innocently) this basic tendency of their makers. Perhaps the most revealing stories of technologically-induced social collapse are those which steer a middle course between these two versions of the myth. In George O. Smith's "Pandora's Millions" (1945) and Damon Knight's *A for Anything* (1959), the invention of matter-duplicators destroy the social order by blasting apart the economic relations which bind it. In the former story civilization is "saved" by the development of a non-duplicatable substance which can function as a medium of exchange—and hence restore Capitalism. In the latter, however, there is no such *deus ex machina*, and the social order is reconstituted, with possessors of the machines establishing themselves as an upper class dominating the lower orders whose sole function is to provide services. The point being made here is that no machine, whatever it does, is likely to be used in a way that benefits all men equally. Machine power is an instrument in social intercourse, and is always likely to be used to create or support inequalities rather than to erode them.

Perhaps the most perfect ironic fantasy in this vein is "E for Effort" (1947) by T. L. Sherred, in which the invention of a device which can "see" through time and space threatens to destroy forever the very possibility of secrecy. No one who enjoys any kind of privilege at all can face this prospect, and when the news of the discovery breaks, there immediately begins a war of man against man, as every power group makes its desperate attempt to corner the use of the machine. By trying to keep it out of the hands of any particular group, the heroes of the story precipitate a war that will destroy mankind.

Stories of this kind *are* essentially ironic, not simply because (as with the Lotus Eater stories) they focus on our inability to withstand fateful temptations, but also because they habitually retain something else from the myth of Epimetheus: the notion that the Pandora's box of invention contains, as well as a host of troubles, such hope as we may legitimately entertain for our future prospects. The machine power which may turn against us also offers us the promise of a better life. The fact that the promise might be so easily betrayed (whether after the fashion of *Paradise and Iron* or "E for Effort") cannot affect the fact that it has been made.

The feeling that underlies these Epimethean fantasies is that machines, one way or another, are getting out of control. We build them to be our servants, and somehow they seem to be threatening to enslave us. Even if we leave aside the potential exploits of artificial intelligence, this feeling is not entirely unrealistic. In the final analysis, political and economic power is dependent upon and shaped by the means of production available to society. It would be overly deterministic to say, with the early Karl Marx, that the hand mill will inevitably generate a feudal system, while the steam mill will generate capitalism; but it is nevertheless true that machines, by making available new means of production, can destroy certain kinds of social structures and greatly encourage others. It is by no means easy to see *what* kind of new social order might emerge from the ultimate triumph of machine production, and very different opinions are offered by various science fiction stories. Knight's *A for Anything*, which envisages a new feudalism, contrasts sharply with Jack Williamson's "The Equalizer" (1947), which foresees an anarchist Utopia emerging from the harnessing of free energy. The major difference between the premises used in the two stories is the simplicity of the machines: in Williamson's story the key to unlimited abundance is available to everyone, but in Knight's novel it is complicated enough to be cornered by the fortunate few. Neither author doubts, though, that it is the nature of the machine, constrained by the happenstance of scientific possibility, which will determine the form of the society which discovers it: the desires of men are impotent.

How impotent the desires and political philosophies of men really are remains open to dispute. There is no doubt, however, that there is sufficient cause for anxiety. It is, indeed, possible that the advancement of technology will bring about great changes in the social order to which we are accustomed, and that we cannot hope to steer a course through those changes exactly as we would wish. Machines do control, at least to some degree, the range of possibilities expressed in our contemporary social evolution, and there can be no guarantee that they will not drive us into an upheaval so great that virtually all of us may consider it catastrophic.

It might be argued that the great failing of twentieth-century science fiction in its dealing with future invention is that it is not *sufficiently* catastrophist. The Epimethean fantasies considered here are, after all, a tiny minority of stories compared with the flood which foresees hardly any changes in the social, political, and economic matrix which surrounds their inventions. On other hand, it might be argued by some that when writers do foresee sweeping changes in social behavior ordained by new technologies, they are too enthusiastic in condemning them as evil by reference to our own transient and artificial value system. After all, leaving aside those fairly unambiguous cases where humanity is wiped out, catastrophe is often in the eye of the beholder. The point at which progress becomes too costly remains a matter for subjective judgment, and there is much lively debate in today's world between those who would place it in the future and those who would place it in the past. The debate has become urgent ever since 1945, when it became clear that technology could—and would—provide nations with the means to bring about that most unambiguous of catastrophes—a war which might annihilate the human race.

5. *Weapons Too Dreadful to Use*

The war-anticipation stories of the period 1871-1914 were, on the whole, quite cheerful and optimistic. War, even fought with airships and submarines, could be seen as a great adventure, and even where it was regarded as an unmitigated evil there was the commonplace assumption that in order to put an end to it, one more final war would have to be fought. The one future war story written before the outbreak of the *real* war which attempts to show in full measure the horrific extent of the misery and destruction that a high-technology war must bring in its train was *The War in the Air* (1908) by H. G. Wells, and even that did not represent the outlook of a whole-hearted catastrophist. Wells feared the next war, but felt that it might do some good in tearing down the fabric of the old social order so that the construction of a new and better one might begin. It is by no means insignificant that his other major future-war novel, featuring the destruction of the world's major cities by atomic bombs, was written on the very eve of the Great War and was titled *The World Set Free* (1914). As the real war began Wells wrote a series of newspaper articles commending it as a marvellous opportunity—these were subsequently collected in the pamphlet, "The War That Will End War" (1914). In 1916 he wrote *Mr. Britling Sees It Through*, a novel providing a moral justification for the war, and he also produced nonfiction works dealing with the reconstruction of the civilization which would follow it. That reconstruction, however, failed to make any headway after 1918, and *The Salvaging of Civilization* (1921) heralded a decline into pessimism that was only occassionally to be alleviated during the remainder of Wells's career. The hope that perhaps the Great War really *had* ended war was steadfastly maintained by a few optimists, but it was really a very feeble hope. Many speculative writers took the view that not only did war remain a possibility, but that it was well-nigh inevitable that it would break out again; and that the only way war would put an end to itself would be in reducing mankind to such a primitive state that he would no longer be capable of waging it.

Before the first world war there had appeared several novels in which scientific supercriminals blackmailed cities, or even the whole world. There had been others in which mad scientists embarked upon careers of spectacular vengeance. Now there was a new fear to set beside these: the fear that by following behavior patterns that were already well-established and quite normal, the politicians of the world might duplicate or surpass the worst that any supercriminal or mad genius might do. It was appreciated that no one would go to war with the deliberate intention of exterminating the human race, but writers now became aware of the possibility of *escalation* which haunted restrained and otherwise local conflicts, and they also became suspicious of the logic of defensive deterrents.

At least one of the contributors to the war-anticipation story repented of what he had done. Erskine Childers, the Irish author of *The Riddle of the Sands* (1903), had espoused in that novel the notion that by being prepared for war Britain might actually preserve herself from war. Later, apparently, he recanted this view. Childers himself was executed in 1922 for his activities supporting the Irish Republican Army, but his nephew added the following note to the 1931 edition of the novel:

> In *The Riddle of the Sands*, first published in 1903, Erskine Childers advocated preparedness for war as being the best preventive for war. During the years that followed, he fundamentally altered his opinion. His profound study of military history, of politics, and later of the causes of the Great War convinced him that preparedness induced war. It was not only that to the vast numbers of people engaged in the fostered war services and armament industries, war meant the exercise of their professions and trades and the advancement of their interests; preparedness also led to international armament rivalries, and bred in the minds of the nations concerned fears, antagonisms, and ambitions, that were destructive to peace.[3]

This perspective, coupled with the knowledge that armaments had already increased in power sufficiently to make the destruction of nations practicable, caused the growth of a new kind of war-anticipation story which was genuinely apocalyptic in its mood.

Edward Shanks's *People of the Ruins* (1920) shows the survivors of a series of crippling wars scratching out a living as scavengers amid the wreckage of civilization, still involved in a constant war of "all against all." *The Collapse of Homo Sapiens* (1923) by P. Anderson

OPENING MINDS, BY BRIAN STABLEFORD

Graham follows the career of a group of refugees hiding from the next war in a shebeen, and goes on to describe the barbarian, science-fearing culture that grows up along the banks of the Thames in a desolated England. In *Ragnarok* (1926) by Shaw Desmond, the survivors of the war live in sewers and caves, fighting against the rats for the means of subsistence, while the surface of the world is devastated by bombs and poison gases. The use of poison gas—the most unselective of weapons—also figures large in scenes of appalling destruction in Neil Bell's *The Gas War of 1940* (1931, as by "Miles"; subsequently retitled *Valiant Clay*), in Ladbroke Black's *The Poison War* (1933), and in Francis Sibson's *Unthinkable* (1933). New and more powerful explosives were also featured extensively: aerial bombing destroys Britain's cities in *The Black Death* (1934) by Moray Dalton and wreaks havoc in *Day of Wrath* (1936) by Joseph O'Neill.

The scale of the destruction envisaged by these stories grew steadily as the second world war approached. Alfred Noyes's *The Last Man* (1940) imagines the nations locked in war having simultaneous recourse to the ultimate weapon, with the result that only a handful of survivors inherit an empty world. The same year saw the first publication of L. Ron Hubbard's *Final Blackout*, a frenetic political fantasy set in a Europe laid waste by the fury of war. In Alfred Bester's "Adam and No Eve" (1941), the destruction is so complete that the only hope for a new beginning lies in the bacteria which multiply in the body of the new "Adam" after his death, and which may perhaps commence the evolutionary story afresh.

The notion that war is too high a price to pay for any political aim or ideology was common in imaginative fiction during the twenties and early thirties. Numerous science fiction stories represented it as the ultimate irrationality—examples include "The Gostak and the Doshes" (1930) by Miles J. Breuer and *In Caverns Below* (also known as *Hidden World*, 1935) by Stanton A. Coblentz. A particularly sharp black comedy is John Gloag's *Tomorrow's Yesterday* (1932), in which a theater company presents a play depicting various stages in the decline and fall of man as a result of war. The play is greeted with hostility and derision and forced to close just as the next war begins. As the thirties proceeded, however, the notion that no price was too dear to pay for the avoidance of war became much less respectable. The Spanish Civil War of 1936 and Hitler's invasion of Czechoslovakia in 1938 re-opened the question of the moral justification of waging war even in the shadow of Armageddon. For this reason, the war-anticipation stories of the late thirties frequently recaptured something of the crusading fervor of those that appeared before the Great War.

The weapon too dreadful to use made its debut on the stage of history in August 1945, its use justified in that it put an end to the second world war, literally at a stroke. The relief brought by the atom bomb was, however, short-lived, for it endorsed in no uncertain terms

THE MYTHOLOGY OF MAN-MADE CATASTROPHE

all the apocalyptic anxieties which had built up in the twenties and thirties. It left no room for doubt that a third world war would be quite capable of destroying the world. Though it was not until 1953, following the advent of the H-bomb, that the U.S. Secretary of Defense announced officially that the U.S. and the U.S.S.R. each had the ability to exterminate the human race, that prospect had been inevitable since 1945. Tales of atomic Armageddon followed in great profusion, the most notable being *Shadow on the Hearth* (1950) by Judith Merril, *The Long Loud Silence* (1952) by Wilson Tucker, *On the Beach* (1957) by Nevil Shute, *Level 7* (1959) by Mordecai Roshwald, and *A Canticle for Leibowitz* (1960) by Walter M. Miller.

The element of black comedy first featured in *Tomorrow's Yesterday* returned in full force in several extraordinarily embittered stories, ranging from Aldous Huxley's *Ape and Essence* (1949) to Peter George's *Dr. Strangelove* (1963). These stories spoke most eloquently to the notion that if the world was bound to end, it was no more than our just desserts. L. Sprague de Camp's "Judgment Day" (1955) is the imaginary biography of a scientific genius whose childhood is a catalogue of miseries. Despite being bullied, harassed, and vilified, he survives to become a brilliant physicist who discovers the secret of the doomsday weapon. He knows that his political masters will use it, but he rejoices in the feeling of vengeful propriety that he experiences in giving it to them. *A Canticle for Leibowitz* is an account of how civilization is put back together after being bombed back into the dark ages, and shows the inexorable process which leads to its bombing itself right back again. Norman Spinrad's "The Big Flash" (1969) recounts the story of a rock band called the Four Horsemen who embody the spirit of their age, and whose climactic concert coincides with the countdown to World War Three. The same author, in *The Iron Dream* (1972), features a science fiction novel written in an alternate universe by a German immigrant to the United States named Adolf Hitler, in which a heroic superman destroys Earth in "saving" it from domination by mutants, but succeeds in sending the seed of his Aryan super-race to the stars. Here science fiction recoils upon itself, striking out at its own mythology and imaginative instruments.

The science fiction community was exultant in 1945, following Hiroshima. The events of history had provided editors, writers, and fans with a golden opportunity to shout, "I told you so!" The same exultancy is obvious in *Ape and Essence*, written by the man whose vision of *Brave New World* had provided a vocabulary of symbols for the adherents of anti-progressive pessimism in the thirties. It was not long before the followers of John W. Campbell realized in a similar fashion that their prophetic victory was in some ways a very bitter one. The pleasure which prophets obtain from being proved right tends to be a rather perverse pleasure when their prophesies carry implications of doom. The prophets of the Christian Millennium had always avoided this perversity well enough by assuming that the end of the old world would be the beginning of the new—salvation for the chosen few, while only the wicked must go to the devil. The prophets of atomic apocalypse, however, had no such escape clause. Radioactive fallout could not be expected to discriminate between the just and the unjust.

It has been argued that our consciousness of the world changed in a fundamental way after 1945—Gunther Anders has claimed that the dictum "all men are mortal" was converted into "all men are exterminable," and that the change was not without consequence in terms of everyday social relationships and political calculations. Whether that is true or not, it is certain that science fiction changed dramatically in its characteristic attitudes, concerns, and methods. Scathing satire and black comedy became common, there was much interest in religious themes which had previously been rigorously excluded, and there was an upsurge of misanthropy which worked wonders for the fortunes of aliens and supermen (who had previously been subject to consistent chauvinistic discrimination). James Blish, in his essay "Cathedrals in Space" (1953), noted that the genre seemed to have become the showcase for a "chiliastic panic" whose like had not been seen since the year 999. In fact, the new situation was rather worse, in that it was now so difficult to believe that disaster might be tempered by the mercy of God. The view of modern man's existence embodied in T. S. Eliot's "The Hollow Men" (1925) persisted, even though it seemed that the world was to end with a bang and not a whimper after all.

Stories of atomic holocaust and its effects are so many and so various that it is difficult to extract from them a consistent opinion regarding the essential flaws in human nature which tend to launch him toward self-destruction. There are, of course, numerous stories which made overt moral points—a notable early example is Theodore Sturgeon's "Thunder and Roses" (1948), which insists that men armed with atom bombs cannot afford the luxury of retaliation—but there are numerous opinions as to which element in human nature warrants the most criticism. There are attacks on militarism, on aggression in general, and on spitefulness. More often than not, however, it is not any *positive* trait in human nature which is stigmatized, but rather a negative one. In the final analysis, what these stories have in common as their fundamental assumption is the argument that we do not—and perhaps cannot—care enough about one another. We are all estranged, and even when we do not find it all too easy to hate one another, we still find it far too difficult to care much one way or the other what happens to people. This is not exactly a new discovery, but only in recent times has it come to be seen as a recipe for catastrophe.

What is perhaps most remarkable about the science fiction of the fifties is neither its conviction that the future will be catastrophic nor its continual recourse to scathing black comedy in its manifold images of unpleasant futures; but rather the nature of the escape route

THE MYTHOLOGY OF MAN-MADE CATASTROPHE

which it found to allow its favored few back to the tollpath to Utopia. It was in the fifties that the mythology of the spaceship really came into its own in science fiction. It was no longer the means to a new and more exciting kind of tourism, but a vital and necessary method of outrunning the terrible destiny of Earthly civilization. If it could blast off for a new Eden, all well and good, but even if it was heading for a hell planet like the Venus of *The Space Merchants* (1953), it was still necessary to get aboard. The reclamation of Earthly society came to be seen, characteristically, as an impossible task. Genre science fiction packed up the future in its kitbag and set off for the stars, while futuristic fiction outside the labelled enclave set about mapping the utter dereliction of our Utopian aspirations. Since 1960 there has been some remission of this condition, as speculative writers have grown more accustomed to the ever-presence of the H-bomb; but so far the forces of moral rearmament visible in the activities of various futurologists and the more technophilic science fiction writers have made little headway in displacing the conviction that every day, in every way, things are getting just a little bit worse.

Looking back on the history of the last hundred years, it is not very difficult to convince ourselves that the tide of progress somehow turned against us during that time. Most people, by inclination if not by nature, are optimists—and in the real world there has been no massive upsurge of despair. The nightmares of popular fiction—and those of not-so-popular fiction even more so—have little more effect on our mundane lives than the haphazard nightmares which visit us in sleep. No matter how seriously one takes stories of atomic holocaust, the effect that they have on one's everyday life is likely to be slight. The exceptions remain exceptional. Nevertheless, the fact that the future now seems threatening to most of us *has* had its effects—notably in refocussing determined optimism on those aspects of life and future possibilities which seem least threatened. In the terms suggested by Frank Manuel, faith in "euchronia"—the better future for society—has evaporated, and has been replaced by faith in "eupsychia"—the possibility that we may (individually or in small groups) achieve a better state of mind. Mysticism has advanced its cause remarkably. So has psychotherapy. So has sex. We are more preoccupied than we have ever been with the problem of getting ourselves straightened out, and the reason is that we have lost all faith in the world getting *itself* straightened out. We have been set on this path since 1945, and it is not easy to see whether we can get off it again in the foreseeable future.

The point of all this is that the advent of atomic weapons did more than confirm a growing suspicion that the modern world possessed the means to bring about a man-made catastrophe of awesome dimensions. It helped bring about a consciousness of the future as a kind of *continuing* catastrophe—a mess which we have already made and would have to take special measures to escape. The lesson of Hiroshima was that *it was already too late* to avoid the dark and hostile future which had earlier been feared; the world was locked on course, and only a few individuals might avoid disaster by locating and occupying boltholes of various kinds. In pursuing this new view of things, the science-fictional imagination has for the last several decades and more, with the active collaboration of many futurologists, discovered a whole host of man-made catastrophes which are already happening.

6. Catastrophe à la Mode

Unlike Dr. Strangelove, most survivors of the second world war did not learn to stop worrying and love the bomb. What *has* happened, however, is that the prospect of atomic war has faded from immediate consciousness into the background of the imagination. There it has merged with a whole series of spectral bugbears which lurk in the shadows of the contemporary image of the future, waiting to devour us as the march of time carries us inexorably into their jaws. We have rediscovered the Malthusian logic of population explosion; we have become painfully aware of the extent to which the wastes of industrial society are poisoning the environment; we have realized how rapidly we are consuming non-renewable resources. In brief, we have begun to come to terms with the built-in obsolescence of the way of life which is followed in the "developed" countries.

When Malthus first published his "Essay on the Principle of Population" in 1798, he was an isolated cynic in an intellectual regime dominated by Enlightenment humanism and an optimistic mythology of progress. His thesis was severely criticized by William Godwin, who felt that human beings could surely rise above the "natural" tendency of populations to increase beyond the limits of their means of subsistence. Malthus was led by this criticism to modify his case, and added to the list of population checks which he had compiled (war, famine, and plague) the notion of conscious population control by "moral restraint."

There is no doubt that Malthus's second thoughts offered a better analysis of the situation than his first. We live today in a world in which strategic action to cope with population growth, on an individual and on a political level, has dramatically changed the pattern of population increase in the developed countries. The means by which this has been achieved are not quite "moral restraints" in the Malthusian sense, but there can be no doubt that the intervention of cultural factors has robbed the tendencies of nature of their deterministic power. It is now obvious that the rate of population increase depends on human choice rather than the tyranny of "natural law." The trouble is that we have come to doubt whether we (or more usually, other people) are making the right choices, or are *capable* of making the right choices.

THE MYTHOLOGY OF MAN-MADE CATASTROPHE

A few science fiction stories of the fifties played with images of an overcrowded world. Cyril M. Kornbluth's "The Marching Morons" (1951) is a black comedy displaying the eventual consequences of the "negative eugenic" trend by which the stupid consistently outbred the wise. Kurt Vonnegut's "The Big Trip Up Yonder" (1954; also known as "Tomorrow and Tomorrow and Tomorrow") envisages the world becoming hopelessly overcrowded because longevity has reduced the death-rate, forcing the return of the extended family to western culture. Frederik Pohl's "The Census Takers" (1956) is a sardonic story of the time when those keeping tally of the population will be required to adjust the actuality to their envisaged ideal. Heavily ironic fables in this vein continued to be produced for another twenty years, until the fashionability of the population explosion began to wane; but they were soon complemented by alarmist stories which took the central Malthusian thesis very much more seriously.

Robert Silverberg's *Master of Life and Death* (1957) follows a critical period in the career of the man responsible for the eugenic decisions which enforce the moral restraint which people are reluctant to supply on their own account. This novel was written in a period when it was still possible to imagine people submitting to laws embodying "scientific rationality." A decade later it was more usual for writers to take a bitter view of the likely outcomes of the democratic process insofar as the politics of population limitation were concerned. The most notable alarmist novels of this period are *Make Room! Make Room!* (1966) by Harry Harrison, *The Wind Obeys Lama Toru* (1967) by Lee Tung, and *Stand on Zanzibar* (1968) by John Brunner. The extremes to which the world might be driven if required to contain a population several orders of magnitude higher than the present one are given detailed consideration in *A Torrent of Faces* (1968) by James Blish and Norman L. Knight and in *The World Inside* (1972) by Robert Silverberg. Draconian alternatives in the matter of population controls administered without the benefit of democratic approval are envisaged in *The Quality of Mercy* (1965) by D. G. Compton, *Logan's Run* (1967) by William F. Nolan and George Clayton Johnson, and "The Pre-Persons" (1974) by Philip K. Dick. The decade within which all of these stories were written was the one in which the population explosion was seen as the principal menace to the future well-being of mankind, though for the latter part of the decade it vied for primacy with the menace which subsequently replaced it: the bugbear of pollution.

Though the fundamental analogy which inspired the new alarmism was taken from science—the fate of yeast-cells confined in a test-tube with an unlimited food supply and their own toxic wastes—the term itself has religious connotations which are by no means out of context when one considers the upsurge of "ecological mysticism" to which this species of alarmism eventually gave birth. The moral tone of the crusades launched in the real world against industrial pollution (which quickly spread to the condemnation of other "ecological sins") has always implied that there are more than mere pragmatic concerns at stake.

In terms of the actual amount of waste materials produced, nineteenth-century factories were frequently far worse than modern ones, and horses rather more profligate than motor cars. The fact that it was not quantity that mattered was first made clear to the world by the publication in 1962 of Rachel Carson's bestselling exposé, *Silent Spring*. Carson pointed out that new organic compounds synthesized for various specific uses were introducing new components into the biosphere. Unlike the poisons manufactured by nature, the new compounds were not biodegradable, and once released into the ecosystem they persisted in living tissues, gradually accumulating in concentration until they reached toxic levels in species at different points in the food-chain. Thus, chlorinated hydrocarbons used as insecticides, like DDT, were gradually being redistributed within the biosphere, threatening fish, birds, and mammals (including man) with a kind of biological time-bomb. Once present, these compounds could not be easily eradicated—and, by an unfortunate stroke of irony, soon lost their effectiveness as pesticides because the insects they attacked, subjected to a ruthless regime of natural selection, quickly developed immunities. Heavy metal pollution, especially involving lead and mercury, also became a special cause for anxiety—where these elements had previously been locked up safely in their inert ores, technological usage was slowly releasing them into the biosphere, where their effects could be—and have been—deadly.

As with overpopulation scare stories, it is possible to find isolated examples of eco-doom stories in the science fiction of the fifties—Cyril M. Kornbluth's "Shark Ship" (1958) is a notable example. The boom in this species of alarmism, however, followed close on the heels of the peak in Malthusian alarmism. The most striking stories of this kind include "We All Die Naked" (1969) by James Blish, "The Lost Continent" (1970) by Norman Spinrad, *The Sheep Look Up* (1972) by John Brunner, *The End of the Dream* (1972) by Philip Wylie, "To Walk With Thunder" (1973) by Dean McLaughlin, and *Brainrack* (1974) by Kit Pedler and Gerry Davis.

As with overpopulation stories, a dominant premise in these extrapolative fantasies is that nothing will be done to prevent disaster until it is too late. Two of the listed stories are apocalyptic in character, while two others look back with ironic approval at the self-destruction of the gluttonous West. McLaughlin's is a particularly subtle political fantasy which suggests that as long as we have technological facilities to combat the direct personal effects of pollution, we will be prepared to put up with it—he is frighteningly plausible in offering an account of the political circumstances which encourage people to permit the poisoning of the atmosphere while the wonders of technology can purify the air supplies to their own homes. The basic argument is that we are insatiable in demanding short-term gratification of even the most puerile of our whims, even if the ultimate consequences will include the suffering of future generations and the death of the earth.

By the time that the new Malthusian crisis and the destruction of the environment had taken their place alongside atomic weapons as seeds of the new apocalypse, other anxieties could fill only a peripheral role. The problem of dwindling resources never became the principal focus of any temporary glut of alarmist science fiction stories, but simply joined the list. So, too, did the gathering anxiety about our psychological and neurological fitness to cope with the pace of change, dubbed "future shock" by well-known futurist Alvin Toffler. Fears of a new economic depression of the kind experienced in the thirties could add no more than a few drops to an ocean of anticipatory tears.

As pollution ceased to be the primary focus of near-future hysteria in science fiction, its place was taken by a much more generalized anxiety. The combined effect of overpopulation and pollution had been given a new name by Paul Ehrlich, who sketched a brief scenario for a nightmare future in "Ecocatastrophe!" (1969); and the notion of a chain-reaction disaster precipitated by a combination of evil circumstances became common. John Brunner's novel, *The Shockwave Rider* (1975), which completed a curious "apocalyptic trilogy," makes use of Toffler's notion of future shock, but the nature of the problematic morass into which its future America is sinking is actually much more elaborate and complex than those featured in *Stand on Zanzibar* and *The Sheep Look Up*.

Science fiction became, in the period when these stories were written, the principal medium by which this pessimistic image of the future was disseminated. Indeed, "non-fictional" speculation and science fiction began to overlap when those engaged in what has come to be known as "futurology" or "futures research" began manufacturing "scenarios" after the fashion of Herman Kahn and Alvin Toffler, and computer simulations of the future after the fashion of the Club of Rome's study of *The Limits to Growth* (1972). The nonfiction, by and large, attempts to make as much use of the sense of tragedy and of hypothetical moral predicaments as does the fiction. ZPG—a movement advocating Zero Population Growth as a political policy for the U.S.— published a science fiction anthology, *Voyages: Scenarios for a Ship Called Earth* in association with Ballantine Books in 1971, which was intended primarily as propaganda. Several futures researchers have produced apologies for science fiction which put a strong case for its use in education. Meanwhile, science fiction writers and editors have been ready enough to accept a didactic role in this connection—other science fiction anthologies which are overtly propagandistic in their alarmism include *Nightmare Age* (1970) edited by Frederik Pohl, *The Ruins of Earth* (1971) edited by Thomas M. Disch, and *Saving Worlds*

(1973, also known as *The Wounded Planet*) edited by Roger Elwood and Virginia Kidd.

Whether science fiction is really effective as an *agent provocateur* inciting the development of a better social conscience is, of course, debatable. It might be suggested that by banishing contemporary (and quite real) social problems to the realms of imaginative fiction, where they take their place alongside invading insects, galactic empires, time travel, and ESP, science fiction is defusing anxieties rather than amplifying them. Final settlement of this question remains a matter for empirical enquiry, but the correlation between the growth of science fictional concern with ecocatastrophe and the growth of concern in the real world does not suggest that the feedback from image to political strategy has been negative. It is much easier to argue the case for a positive feedback.

Some commentators have found it difficult to reconcile the argument that these visions of man-made catastrophe have a constructive role to play with the fact that so many of them are characterized by black despair and a conviction of hopelessness. (The same, incidentally, is true of many futurological speculations, which claim that it is already too late for any action to be really effective—a cardinal example is *Delivrez Prométhée* (1979) by Jérôme Deshusses.) In reply, the immediate temptation is to recover the argument used by Joad in his essay of 1930, to the effect that speculators have a duty to be as pessimistic as possible in order that they "may hope to irritate...readers sufficiently to provoke them to make the efforts necessary to prove [their] predictions false." Often, however, the arguments used in these stories are so completely nihilistic that it is difficult to construe them as anything other than exhortations to complete passivity. This is especially true of those science fiction stories which contain an element usually missing from futurological speculations—the element of jeering black comedy. Robert Silverberg's story of imaginary tourist trips to colorful apocalypses, launched from a near future which is dying its own sordid death, "When We Went to See the End of the World" (1972) is one of the more subtle examples; Kurt Vonnegut's "The Big Space Fuck" (1972) is surely the most bitterly hysterical. In their account of the "human nature" which precipitates catastrophe, these stories not only leave no room for hope, but suggest that if hope *did* exist it would be a violation of common justice.

In so many science-fictional catastrophe stories of the last two decades we are urged to believe that we deserve every last moment of the suffering that we are bringing upon ourselves. It will, it is presumed, constitute an adequate payment for our sins, even though it will not constitute an expiation. Only a tiny minority of stories actually carry this "message" in manifest form, and many more reject it insistently, but the very fact that it exists at all is a matter of considerable significance; and it is, indeed, no more than the logical extreme of the

The Mythology of Man-Made Catastrophe

line of argument taken by all the fiction which accepts the image of an ecologically sick future.

The true measure of the despair which has begun to gnaw at the heart of the image of the future contained within science fiction is not so much to be found in the violence of its images of destruction, but in the way that the accusing finger which seeks to allocate blame so frequently leaves no exceptions. In stories written before 1945, whether they deal with lotus eater societies or future wars, the allocation of responsibility is usually selective. For the most part, the clear-sighted, middle-class intelligentsia are absolved of blame—it is the power groups above them or the lower orders below whose greedy short-sightedness precipitates disaster. As most of the writers of these stories were members of the middle-class intelligentsia who saw their work as an attempt to send out warning signals, this exemption is not altogether surprising. After the war, however, attitudes changed markedly. The supposed moral neutrality of scientists came under suspicion, and the scientists had always seemed to represent the ideological spearhead of the intelligentsia. When the pollution crisis became dominant among the anxieties of the period, the culpability of the intelligentsia as a whole could no longer be doubted, for it was in maintaining the standard of living expected by the middle-classes that industrialism was threatening to run riot and poison the earth. To some extent, therefore, the absolutism of the note of despair sounded in some of these stories represents a kind of self-abuse on the part of speculators who have come to see themselves as active participants in the catastrophe they anticipate. Andrew J. Offutt, in his ecocatastrophe story, *The Castle Keeps* (1972), quotes with approval the words of the comic-strip character Pogo: "We have met the enemy, and he is us!"—a comment which is highly pertinent in both a general and a special sense.

When we bear this fact in mind, it becomes easier to see why the note of despair sounded by the more extreme apocalyptic fantasies does not destroy the possibility of their filling a constructive role. As evangelical rabble-rousers discovered a long time ago, it pays to reduce your audience to despair by convincing them of their personal damnation before attempting to win them to the cause with conditional promises of salvation. It is a tried-and-true recipe for making converts (though the treatment must periodically to be renewed, lest they lapse). The whole point about the eclectic catastrophism which is so prominent in contemporary science fiction is that it is not a warning about what *they* might do to us if we let them, but a warning about what we are doing to ourselves. The scapegoat strategy by which we try to pin blame to other individuals or groups, to other people's ideas, or to facets of "human nature" which we have risen above while others cannot, seems (at long last) to be going out of fashion.

7. "What Is Sin?"

The question "What is sin?" is asked by Felix Hoenikker in Kurt Vonnegut's *Cat's Cradle* (1963), when one of his colleagues wonders (after the fashion of J. Robert Oppenheimer) whether the invention of the atom bomb constitutes the scientists' sin. Hoenikker is a scientist through and through, and all his concepts are scientific ones. The concept of sin is not among them. For him, all problems are theoretical, and have no moral dimension. Thus, when he is asked to find a way to freeze battlefields so that soldiers will not have to fight in mud, he does so. His invention, ice-9, will also freeze the entire world if a single drop ever escapes into the environment, but that is a problem which he leaves for his children (and, indeed, for all the world's children) to cope with. In the end—which, of course, really *is* the end—they *can't* cope.

Cat's Cradle is exceptional among modern stories of manmade catastrophe because it sets against the hopelessness of our envisaged situation a very powerful note of pity. The irony of our impending self-destruction is allowed full rein; there is no doubt expressed within the story that we are getting pretty much what we deserve. Nevertheless, argues Vonnegut, we are to be pitied in our plight. It is this element of pity, also strongly expressed in *Mother Night, God Bless You, Mr. Rosewater*, and *Slaughterhouse-5*, which makes Vonnegut a unique figure in modern American literature. Those who recognize that the hopelessness of his stories is a kind of self-abuse are apt to construe the pity as self-pity, and are generally antipathetic in consequence; but it is not difficult to see why his attitude has seemed so attractive to those who have made Vonnegut a cult figure. In Vonnegut's books we are all *responsible* for the coming catastrophe, but there remains a special sense in which we are nevertheless innocent. We are victims of samaritrophia (chronic degeneration of the conscience), but it is not really our fault—we are embarked upon a curious kind of "children's crusade."

The ideology opposed to Hoenikker's morally-blind scientific rationalism in *Cat's Cradle* is Bokononism, a mock religion which boasts of its falseness, but claims that belief in its tenets is pragmatically essential because life is otherwise intolerable. Vonnegut echoes Voltaire in observing that since God does not exist, it is necessary for us to invent him, and adds that we should not let the manifest absurdity of the project deter us in the least. Ice-9 will get us anyway, but there is a chance that some of us, at least, can go out thumbing our noses at the utterly indifferent universe which has sealed our fate.

This kind of catastrophist comedy re-emphasizes the message transmitted by catastrophist tragedy. (This is not surprising, in that the common subject matter of comedy and tragedy is failure—they merely represent different attitudes to human fallibility.) The argument is that we have failed our children and our children's children, and in so doing we have failed ourselves. We are no longer required to believe that death will deliver us into purgatory or hell for our due punishment, but there remains a special sense in which we can be—and are—damned.

It could be argued that the sins which figure large in modern stories of man-made catastrophism are not so very different from the sins identified by our remote ancestors. Pride, covetousness, sloth, and gluttony still make convenient labels to use in connection with Epimethean fantasies, the modern versions of the lotus eater mythology, and anticipations of drowning in our own wastes. Mythical parallels are not only easy to draw but rather difficult to avoid. However, there is one vital, and perhaps all-important, difference between the concept of sin which is revealed and propagandized by modern accounts of man-made catastrophe and the concept which figures in the Bible and other ancient mythologies. The character of the sins, insofar as they reveal human propensities for antisocial behavior, has not changed, but the essential nature of sin itself has.

Our ancestors saw sin in the context of a static order of nature. They conceived of it as a violation of that order—a rebellion against it which would (or, at least, should) call down retribution. Because it was seen as a violation of some kind of rigid framework, sin was held to be *unnatural*. The tendency to sin might be universal—and, indeed, all men might be tainted by it even if they never actually committed any sins of their own, but sin was nevertheless a flaw in human nature from which men could (or, at least, should) be redeemed. The Christian mythology of sin is particularly clear in this respect, but this kind of attitude is one of the things which is common to all religious systems.

We no longer see sin as a violation of a natural order, but as part of it. The human propensities which seem to propel individuals and societies toward disaster are now seen to be a *part* of human nature rather than a flaw distorting it. This change of perspective, of course, became inevitable once we realized that we are the product of evolution rather than special creation. We are what circumstances have made us, and what is common to us all must be accepted as a part of what we are, not as an accidental deterioration which we suffered after our essential nature was determined. This recognition does not, of course, rule out the possibility of redemption, for if we are the product of past evolution, then future evolution might remake us more as we would like to imagine ourselves; but it makes the process of redemption a much more difficult business than we had ever suspected.

The rationalistic philosophy of science claims that knowledge itself is morally neutral, and that the question of what *is* must be separated from the question of what *ought to be*. However, we must observe that even if science does not actually *contain* a moral philosophy, it nevertheless determines what kind of moral philosophy *can* exist. It denies validity to any moral philosophy which seeks to validate its commandments by embedding them in empirical claims, whether such empirical claims are true or false. It catches religious mythologies in a double stranglehold, making their claims false in the simple sense where they are genuine empirical claims, and falsely empirical if they are metaphysical in nature.

The result of this is that the only kind of morality which can genuinely co-exist with and complement systematic scientific knowledge is a pragmatic one, which makes the desirability of ends the sole criterion for the assessment of means. The true beauty of this is that the instrument by which we seek to calculate the outcome of our present policies in order to discover the ends which we must weigh up, and by which we also seek to extend the repertoire of our available actions in order to widen the *range* of our possible ends, is scientific knowledge itself. Thus, though a pragmatic moral philosophy can make no claim to *be* science, it nevertheless depends for its potency entirely upon the competence of science. It is no use trying to evaluate an action by its consequences unless you actually have the means of calculating its consequences. Pragmatism cannot exist without science, and science is useful (and hence attractive) only in a pragmatic sense.

The essence of sin, in the age of science, is to be a bad scientist—which is say, to fail to calculate correctly (and hence to realize fully) the consequences of one's actions. This becomes, in fact, the very nature of sin in a wholly pragmatic world. It seems at first to be a rather harsh and simple-minded doctrine, in that the cardinal sin then becomes stupidity, and the register of deadly sins becomes a list of different kinds of stupidity. The true situation is, however, more complicated than this, though we have perhaps only recently begun to realize the fact.

In the prewar mythology of man-made catastrophe investigated in this essay, it is true that the ultimate crime, however it is characterized, is a form of stupidity. The stories of lotus-eater societies are perhaps the best example, for what those societies are seen to have abandoned is progress, foresight, and the use of intelligence. What has atrophied in such societies is precisely the capacity to make plans and to set up new goals. In the anti-war stories war is very frequently represented explicitly as a kind of stupidity or a kind of irrationality. If one studies the impassioned speeches made by the sympathetic characters in these stories, while they survey the wreckage of civilization or watch it collapsing about them, there can be no mistaking the consistent indictment of stupidity, and the taken-for-granted belief that if only the world were run intelligently and rationally everything would be all right. In catastrophist stories written outside the science fiction magazine community, the intelligentsia were generally held immune from criticism, though the characterization of the class differs somewhat between, say, H. G. Wells and Aldous Huxley. In stories and novels actually labelled science fiction, there was greater consensus on this matter, in that the intelligentsia were more exclusively those educated *in science*.

As we have seen, however, this exemption is made far less frequently in postwar catastrophe stories. There are few people today who could commit themselves to the Wellsian ideal of a state run by technocrats. Stupidity may still be the essence of sin, but we have lost faith in rationality as the over-riding virtue.

The reason for this is simple enough. It is all very well for scientific knowledge to function (through technology) as the means of extending our repertoire of actions, and hence of options, and to be the instrument by which we may calculate the consequences of our proposed actions. The trouble is that none of this will help us to decide exactly which ends *are* desirable and which are not. The nineteenth-century rationalists would have been unable to perceive a problem: here man, as the product of evolution, was considered to have his desires "built in" to his nature, and the Utilitarians were quite confident of their ability to add up social equations in terms of "hedonic units" of one kind or another. Even the Utilitarians, however, began to find practical difficulties when they began to weigh up immediate personal gratifications against long-term policies which would generate hedonic satisfactions only for future generations.

Obviously, it would be oversimplifying the case to say that postwar catastrophists discovered this problem, or even that they rediscovered it. What they *have* done, however, is to realize its immediate and urgent significance. For what they are saying, in essence, is that *our* sin consists of gambling with the happiness of future generations in the pursuit of immediate gratification for ourselves. They say further—and quite rightly—that the intelligent are more to blame in this sense than the stupid, for it is they that have the means to do it. Thus, sin is balanced against sin, and there *is* a curious sense in which, though are all responsible, we are each in our different ways innocent.

It can readily be seen that this new sin, though it is different from the sin of stupidity, is still a sin in the pragmatic sense of the word. It is still a sin of *consequences*, not of violation of nature. It reveals the unanswered question which underlies all pragmatic philosophy: how far must I take my calculation of consequences before pausing to evaluate their desirability? In a crude sense, it has always been known to moral and political philosophers as the question of how much I can take into account benefits which accrue to me if the actions which generate them cause hardship to others. The fact that in cases of man-made catastrophe the others I am forced to worry about include my own children adds a measure of poignancy to the question, but does not alter its character to any great extent.

The main reason why the question seems to be renewed and reinvigorated in these contemporary versions is precisely because the advance of science—the instrument of pragmatism—has ensured that the consequences of our present-day collective actions are so much greater, and that we are better able to calculate them. Along with a greater ability to make disasters has come a greater ability to foresee them. It is this second ability which has generated the immense wealth of recent catastrophist nightmares, but the fact that the stories themselves are "science fiction," making use of techniques of extrapolation in order to make predictions which (we fear) may be too late to overturn, should not be allowed to distract us from the fact that the problem which they pose for us is not a technical problem, but a moral one. In a way, this is a shame, because technical problems have solutions which are "already there," waiting only to be found. If moral problems have "solutions" at all, they have to be created, not merely discovered.

Whether we are "naturally" incapable of such collective creative effort is open to doubt, but one thing is certain: we haven't had much practice.

If we really are going to fail the examination to which circumstances are currently subjecting the human race, that will be the reason.

VII.

THE PLAUSIBILITY OF THE IMPOSSIBLE

We are all familiar with deceptive illusions. We know how easily our eyes are fooled by drawings of impossible objects such as those which feature the designs of M. C. Escher: the staircases which are always ascending although the top of every flight connects mysteriously with the bottom of another; the belvedere whose columns appear to be straight, although they connect with the wrong corners of the building. If we look through a window into an Ames distorting room where identical twins stand in the far corners, one twin seems to be very much taller than the other. If we watch a person move from one corner of an Ames room to another (as the members of the group Squeeze do in their "Hourglass" video), they seem to us to grow or shrink in size. We know on a cognitive level, that the Escher belvedere could not exist, but our eyes cannot identify any single point in the picture where the lie has been built in. We are perfectly certain that the people moving across the Ames room cannot really be changing size, but our eyes still insist that the room is normal and the people are not.

Such confusions as these arise because seeing is not a passive process; sight is partly interpretation. When we look at an Escher drawing or a photograph taken in an Ames room, we read the third dimension into the image by inference. We may do this by noting overlaps, or by observing the effects of perspective, which make parallel lines seem to converge.

In the Ames room, of course, the angles of the room are not right angles, and its lines are not parallel. The corner where one twin stands is much more distant than the other one where the other stands. Our eyes, however, literally cannot see this difference in distance because the design of the room compensates for the effects of perspective. The assumption that rooms contain right-angles has become accepted, at a fundamental level, into the interpretative process by which we see, so that when we look into an Ames room we are able to see something which we know, at the cognitive level, to be impossible. The impossible has been made plausible.

As well as *plausible* impossibilities, there are also implausible possibilities, which are the stock-in-trade of conjurors. Conjurors, like the designers of optical illusions, exploit the inferences which we tend to draw as we see things. By allowing us to see only that from which we will draw the wrong inferences, they cause us to infer that the coin is in one hand when it is really in the other, or that the lady in the box has been sawn in half.

What the conjuror has done we know to be possible, because he has just done it, but we are usually quite mystified as to *how* it has been done, because he has clearly made it implausible. Dishonest conjurors, representing themselves as real magicians, spiritualist mediums, or psychic metal-benders, have since time immemorial tried to convince others that the implausibility of what they have done proves the involvement of some kind of occult power.

Human beings rely very heavily on the sense of sight. "Seeing is believing," we say; whereas we are rather more likely to speak sceptically of "hearing things." If we see something happen, it really does *command* belief; by the same token, if we did not see where the coin or the elephant went, it is genuinely difficult to believe that it did not simply disappear into thin air when the illusionist waved his wand.

The primacy of sight in the human sensorium, and the trust we habitually put in it, opens up extravagant scope for the willing suspension of disbelief, which is most spectacularly evident in animated cartoons. The two-dimensional world of the animated cartoon is manifestly different from the two-dimensional world photographed by the movie camera. A frame of time and space is loosely mapped onto it, but the limits of possibility within that frame are determined by the artist's pen, which is in some ways much more limited than a camera, and in others much less. Animators cannot produce a simulacrum of real life, but they can depict mice which walk on their hind legs, wear clothes, and talk in funny voices. We can see these creatures, and we are quite ready to believe in them while they are in their own parallel world (but if such creatures appear in our world, we can see perfectly well that they are only people in silly costumes).

In their own world, cartoon characters can do all kinds of things which no one could do in ours. They can be squashed like pancakes by boulders, rebound like concertinas, and then right themselves with a shrug of the shoulders. If they run into a brick wall they can go clean through it, leaving a hole shaped like a silhouette. If they run off the edge of a cliff they will not begin to fall until they actually notice that there is nothing beneath their feet. All these things are enabled to become conventional visual jokes because of the plausibility conferred on them by our willingness to learn a new set of conventions appropriate to the perception of this alternative world. Because we are dealing with a manifestly different world, the process of negotiation which goes on between the animator and the viewer is much less vexed than the similar process involving cinematic special effects combined with live-action photography, where plausibility can easily be lost if the monster is too obviously a man in a furry suit or a cardboard cut-out.

The Plausibility of the Impossible

I would like to extend this argument, if I can, from consideration of the plausibility of visual images to a more general consideration of the plausibility of ideas. I think this is interesting, because it may help us to see how certain stereotyped themes have become acceptable in imaginative fiction. Imaginative fiction deals, almost by definition, with the impossible, but if it is to be effective it must deal with plausible impossibilities, and impossibilities cannot be made plausible at random.

There is some imaginative fiction which claims that it does not deal with impossibilities, most of it belonging to the sub-species called science fiction. In fact, though, science fiction has always played host to certain ideas which, within the world-view of contemporary physics, we have every reason to judge impossible. The three most conspicuous examples are time-travel, faster-than-light travel, and the various psychic powers usually lumped together as psi-powers or ESP. Unpacking these notions leads to logical contradictions, or to blatant defiance of fundamental laws, or at the very least to a complete absence of any hypothetically-definable mechanism. In order to accommodate them, the serious-minded SF writer must make very radical amendments to the assumed universe of his story; nevertheless, their use is widely sanctioned because the ideas have an innate attractiveness—they have a plausibility which is independent of any rational consideration of their possibility.

For many people, of course, the plausibility of an idea can be powerful enough to override rational considerations of possibility, even to the extent of commanding actual belief. ESP is one such example, and it is interesting that there are several other such notions which continue to command belief among the credulous, though they are disqualified from any significant place in science fiction. Ghosts, bloodthirsty pagan gods, reincarnations, and ritual magic are all virtually taboo in science fiction, but some of these notions still command a measure of real belief, and all are part of the staple diet of horror fiction and heroic fantasy.

Clearly, the writers and readers who are the users of the various sub-species of imaginative fiction enter into different tacit contracts regarding suspension of disbelief. Different criteria of plausibility apply in different genres, but I think that significant analogies can be drawn between the determinants of plausibility in all these cases, and the determinants which apply to the plausibility of such optical illusions as the Ames room. In every instance, I believe, the plausibility of an impossibility arises out of the fact that perception and experience are inherently interpretative; this applies to perception of ourselves as well as perception of the world in which we find ourselves.

We must remember that the universe which we have discovered by means of the scientific method is in certain important respects implausible. It defies common sense—by which, in this instance, I mean the inferences which we commonly find convenient in ordinary sensory experience. The understanding of distance which we get from the sense of sight makes inches and feet easy to cope with, miles slightly harder, and light-years virtually unimaginable. The horizon which we see is rarely more than a few miles away, and that fact defines the size of our perceptual universe. Our *con*ceptual universe was always greater than that, but the further it extends into the macrocosm and the microcosm the more difficult that universe is to grasp imaginatively. There is nothing plausible about the transactions of subatomic particles which are defined by quantum mechanics, and for a being with three-dimensional senses it is a tremendous imaginative endeavor to conceive of a universe which is a four-dimensional Riemannian hypersphere. Such things are certainly possible, and what we deduce from evidence leads us to believe that they are true, but plausible they are not.

To imagine the galaxy, as SF writers frequently do, as if it were a kind of archipelago, with habitable worlds among which interstellar travellers could commute, is an absurdity; but it is only by such an act of crude reduction that our minds, attuned to environments perceptible to the human sensorium, can attempt to compass or get to grips with the idea of the galaxy. In more honest representations of the galaxy, we must use mathematical representations of raw data whose meanings are rigorously controlled by logic, but which are very difficult for the mind to get hold of. Science fiction aspires towards a realistic mode of representation, but can never really get there; it claims to be mind-stretching, and indeed it is in a perfectly literal sense, for what it tries to do in getting to grips with the cognitively-known universe is to make our minds more elastic—but the imaginatively "seen" universe will always be a very mediocre thing by comparison with the cognitively-known universe.

As in the case of the Ames room, there is a manifest conflict between what I know cognitively, thanks to scientific discovery, and what I can "see" in what is aptly described as "the mind's eye." I *know* that the universe is extremely large, but when I try to imagine it, all I can picture is the kind of tourist-brochure galactic civilization which is common and conventional in science fiction. I also know that it is impossible to travel faster than light, but in my mind's eye I have not the slightest difficulty in picturing starships making the journey from Earth to Alpha Centauri in a matter of days. By the same token, although I *know* that human beings could not be shrunk to microscopic size without their cells and organs becoming incapable of functioning, I have little difficulty in imagining what the world would look like from that hypothetical viewpoint, and hence in reading or watching microcosmic romances.

Other interesting conventions of plausibility arise when the "mind's eye" tries to look back on itself. Perceiving ourselves is much more problematic than perceiving the world out there, because the mind is essentially invisible. The mind is much more difficult to pin down and examine than the entities which we perceive in the world around us—even those entities invisible to the naked eye.

Without setting aside Kantian doubts about the extent to which the phenomenal world of things as they seem differs from the noumenal world of things as they are, we can easily accept that a building or a rhinoceros is not *too* difficult to describe. We can not only talk about its shape, its color, and its texture, but about the different sorts of bits it is made of, and how those bits fit together into a functioning whole. The mind has none of these properties, and the properties which it does seem to have are curiously deceptive. Attempts made by philosophers to describe the mind do not easily stand up to rigorous examination.

The Cartesian mind—that ghostly entity of mental substance which sat in the pineal body pulling the levers which controlled the body-machine—is easily revealed by rigorous criticism to be a sham; but that really is how we appear to ourselves when we attempt to examine ourselves from within. The Cartesian mind is impossible, but it is seductively plausible. It is not just that it is easy for me to "picture" myself as if I were a ghost in a fleshy machine, but that it is extremely difficult for me to picture myself any other way.

This way of imagining the mind carries with it certain corollaries which—though no more rationally possible than the Cartesian ghost-in-the-machine itself—partake of its aura of plausibility. These corollaries include the rather exciting notion that the mind might exist, and seem not much different, outside the body or after the body's death. More anxious corollaries include the notion that another mind might invade my body, displacing, imprisoning, or enslaving the Cartesian me.

If we abandon the task of trying to make the mind into a whole graspable entity and concentrate more narrowly on its particular attributes, the situation is no clearer. I can make pseudo-visual images inside my head: mental pictures. I can produce thoughts in words, and talk to myself without making any sound. The idea that these mental pictures are potentially able to be "seen" by other minds or my thoughts in words overheard by a mental eavesdropper lends a powerful plausibility to the idea of telepathy, though of course the pictures are not really seeable and the thoughts in words not really audible.

Then again, if I study my mind's power of control over itself, I can hardly help but be drawn—as Spinoza was in the most fundamental propositions in his rationalist account of the mind—to the notion that my own authority over myself is compromised and undermined by the impulses and urges which we usually call emotions. It is very difficult for the mind, contemplating itself, to resist the notion that it is the focal point of a conflict between a higher and a baser nature, whether we speak of reason and emotion, or id and superego, or guardian angels and tempting demons, or of the struggle of noble purposes against animal instincts. This lends plausibility to many kinds of images of divided selves: victims of demonic possession, werewolves, spilt personalities. It lends plausibility to hypothetical forces which can take hold of us as passionate emotions seem to do: to geases, curses, and love potions.

Yet again, if I study myself as a being in time, I appear to myself as a traveller in time. I can, by a mental effort, project my self into tomorrow or bring back yesterday. I can anticipate, anxiously testing out possibilities, what I am going to say in tomorrow's interview. I can remember not only what I did say but what I should have said in that embarrassing conversation I had yesterday; I know not only the line of reasoning which led me to bet on the wrong horse in the big race, but also what line of reasoning might have led me to the right one. Nor do I have much difficulty in savoring, in the imagination, the successful interview, the conversational coup, and the winning of the bet. In our minds, we can bind time to our pleasure, reconstructing the past, and anticipating the future. Small wonder that we find stories of time travel and alternative history both plausible and powerfully appealing.

All these plausible impossibilities are parasitic upon the interpretations which we make when we try to understand what it is we mean when we speak of our "selves," following the perspectives of the mind's eye. They do not stand up to rational analysis any better than the idea of the galactic archipelago or the atomic solar system, but there is a significant difference between the effects of rational analysis on our understanding of the world without and its effects on our understanding of the world within.

The universe which scientific analysis reveals to us might be implausible and difficult to grasp, but at least we have an image of sorts—something that the language of mathematics can describe and make sense of. But the rational arguments which reveal the absurdity of the Cartesian self put no other self in its place; they leave nothing but a vacuum of understanding unfilled by describable possibilities, however implausible. Our confrontation with ourselves remains, therefore, unresolved and uneasy, and our relationship with such plausible impossibilities as the Cartesian ghost is a troubled one.

This uneasiness affects the fictions which we make up. I do not mean by this that there can be no happy fantasies of benign ghosts whose visitations have good results, or power fantasies in which the hero's ability to read the minds of others enables him to win against the odds; but the general rule is bound to be that tales which take their warrant from our perceptions of our own inner being are undercut by doubt and anxiety, and a sense of the impossibility of ultimately making sense of things. Modern horror stories, from the Gothic novel on, have liberally exploited this sensibility.

Because the plausible impossibilities which arise from our perception of ourselves carry this unease, robustly uplifting fantasies are very frequently transplanted into worlds displaced in some curious parallel dimension—Secondary Worlds, in Tolkienesque jargon. When supernatural stories notionally set in our world have happy endings, it is usually because a *personal* threat has been averted, and sometimes there can be no such escape. In heroic fantasy, by contrast, the threat is usually to the whole world, the conclusion is the salvation of the world, and it is very rare indeed that such salvation is refused.

The secondary worlds of heroic fantasy are more like the world of animated cartoons than the synthetic realities of conventional cinematography—a fact realized by the few film-makers who have been interested in the genre, and by the authors who have found heroic fantasy the natural modern medium for talking-animal stories. Secondary worlds are worlds where the ground-rules have been redefined, and it is no coincidence that the redefinition often mimics very closely the world-views embraced by preliterate societies. Just as preliterate man attempted to superimpose his perception of himself upon his perception of the world, animating that world with ghost-spirits and credulously embracing the notion of magical control, so the literary creator of a Secondary World converts his perceived inner reality into an outer reality. Here, in place of a divided self we have a divided world where Good and Evil or Order and Chaos are essentially at odds, where moral questions replace scientific ones as the fundamental instruments of analysis, where allegorical interpretations of events are frequently intended and always viable. (We see this most obviously in the Thomas Covenant stories of Stephen R. Donaldson, where the correspondence between the Secondary World and the protagonist's inner world is made explicit.)

Of course, the Secondary Worlds of heroic fantasy are impossible; there is no conceivable space in which they can exist—but of course they are plausible too, to the remarkable extent that they can command in their users an involvement and an allegiance more intimate and more passionate than any merely real world ever could. If, when we are reading a heroic fantasy, we find plausibility threatened, it is more likely to be the case that the author has borrowed with reckless ineptitude from history or mythology than that he has offended our sense of propriety with his own inventions. Secondary worlds command plausibility because they offer us landscape and politics which render incarnate key features of the Cartesian mind—the mind as it appears to the "mind's eye."

In summary, what I have tried to argue here is this: that plausibility is governed by the interpretations which are inbuilt into our ways of perceiving—inbuilt, that is, into our sensory perceptions of the world without and our introspective perceptions of the world within.

When impossible things become plausible, it is because interpretations which cannot stand up to rigorous rational criticism continue to hold their dominion over the imagination, which they do because we have no resources to draw upon which would allow them to be replaced. The cultivation of reason has led us inescapably to the conclusion that we are implausible entities who exist in an implausible universe.

It is, I believe, because we are implausible entities adrift in that implausible universe that we need fantasies—and I mean the word "need" in a strong sense, though fictions produced by artists and writers are by no means the only sources which feed that need, and it is only in the recent past that writers of fantastic fictions have enjoyed significant success in reclaiming their proper role from more ambitious pretenders—theologians and other mystics. Fantastic fictions are instruments of negotiation with which we try to accomplish the difficult diplomacy of existence in a scientifically knowable but essentially unimaginable world. The politics of escapism involve a series of retreats into cognitively manageable "environments," where we might find all manner of dreadful monsters, but where we can at least face those monsters honestly.

It is because we are the particular kinds of implausible entities that we are, adrift in the particular kind of implausible world in which we find ourselves, that we have developed the particular genres and sub-species of imaginative fiction which have grown in close association with the progress of reason and science. Science fiction, horror, and fantasy, despite the very different metaphysical assumptions which they seem to make, are bound together into a common enterprise: they are those defenders of human plausibility which do not fear to employ the impossible as a means.

VIII.

MARXISM, SCIENCE FICTION, AND THE POVERTY OF PROPHECY: SOME COMPARISONS AND CONTRASTS

Karl Marx was not a prophet. He did not regard the prediction of the future to be his primary aim. Nevertheless, he did have a good deal to say about future possibility and about the fate of the capitalist economic system. Many Marxists are reluctant to concede that Marx is really vulnerable to the charges brought against him by Karl Popper in the chapters of *The Open Society and Its Enemies* which deal with "Marx's Prophecy," but however just or unjust it may be to condemn Marx on the grounds of prophetic failure it is the case that Marx's ideas about the future are of some interest. It is also the case that Popper's attempt to analyze the question of why Marx failed to produce a competent picture of future developments is of some interest as a particular case of a general argument about the impossibility of prediction.

Science fiction is not prophetic either, despite the claims made by some of its early apologists—especially Hugo Gernsback. When we compare today's world with the many images of life in the 1990s contained in science fiction stories written many years ago, we can easily see that no one came remotely close to accurate anticipation. Because most of this antique SF made no claim to intellectual seriousness in the first place hardly anyone bothers to raise the question of why the writers were so completely wrong. Even where intellectual seriousness was a factor—as, for instance, in George Orwell's *Nineteen Eighty-Four*—it was not predictive seriousness, and commentators on such works are right not to waste their time in discussing the reasons why the real 1984 does not much resemble Orwell's. Nevertheless, the poverty of science-fictional prophecy is of some interest with respect to Popper's arguments about the impossibility of prediction.

Popper's comments on the futuristic dimension in Marx's thought are held by their author to be a test of Marx's theory—a test which, in Popper's view, Marx fails. it requires only a shift of perspective, though, to allow us to consider these comments as a test of Popper's theory of prophetic poverty. From this viewpoint the relevant question is whether Popper has correctly explained why Marx's expectations were bound to be betrayed. It will help, of course, if we can

99

confront Popper's theory with some other sets of expectations too, in order to see how it copes with the task of accounting for *their* betrayal. This is why it should prove illuminating to compare and contrast the anticipations of Marx with the anticipations of science fiction writers.

Though it should need no emphasis, it may be as well to state flatly at this point that the poverty of the art of prophecy is not in dispute. No one can reasonably doubt that all attempts to foresee the course of future history have failed miserably. The question to be raised in this essay is *why* these attempts have always failed, and whether Popper's particular account of the impossibility of anticipation is the correct one.

Popper's principal work dealing with the impossibility of anticipation is *The Poverty of Historicism*. Although this was not published in book form in English until 1957 the thesis which it contains dates back to 1919-20, and was first commited to print in three articles published in 1944-45.[1] The evaluation of Marx's prophecies in *The Open Society and Its Enemies*—first published in 1945—follows fairly closely the main argument of *The Poverty of Historicism*.

According to this main argument, Marx's prognoses regarding the future evolution and ultimate fate of capitalism were mistaken because they erroneously assumed that certain "historical tendencies" or trends were actually laws of social development. Popper suggests that human scientists of the "historicist" persuasion believe that there are "laws of succession" which dictate the progress of patterns of social change.[2] Popper asserts that there are no such laws of succession at all, in any branch of science.

Actually, it is not altogether clear that the distinction between trends and laws is as radical as Popper makes it out to be; nor is it beyond dispute that there are no laws of succession at all. It is true that laws of succession in human science—for instance, Grimm's law, which deals with shifts in consonants during the development of the Indo-European languages—are pretty shoddy examples of scientific laws, but *all* the so-called laws in human science are pretty shoddy, and it is not simply the fact that some of them aspire to be laws of succession that makes them so. It is true, too, that natural science has not many laws of succession, and that the ones in biology—for instance, Haeckel's law, usually stated as "ontongeny recapitulates phylogeny"— are far from convincing. On the other hand, such laws of succession in physics as the half-life equations which describe the decay of radioactive elements seem reliable enough as instruments of prediction.

Even if we set aside these reservations, though, it remains highly dubious that human scientists—Marx included—really do confuse trends and laws in a naïve fashion, and that their anticipations of the future are silly *for this reason*. T. R. Malthus, whose first *Essay on Population* (1798) did refer to the tendency of human population to increase geometrically as if this were a law, but he was quickly led by

Marxism, SF, and the Poverty of Prophecy

criticism offered by William Godwin and others to revise his view. In the second edition of 1803 he agreed that this tendency might be defeated by voluntary moral restraint, so that the trend might be turned aside. It is not easy to find examples after 1803 of human scientists who fell into the kind of trap that Malthus fell into in the first essay.

Of course, human scientists often have devoted a good deal of attention to historical trends—examples which figure large in social theory include the progressive accumulation of knowledge, the trend in Western European society toward secularization, and the increasing division of labor. Theorists have often tried to show how these trends are related to one another, and how they assist in the generation of other aspects of social change. It is not clear, though, that social scientists have frequently referred to such trends as laws in any other than a metaphorical sense. (What is more, *these* trends have continued, and if social scientists have mistakenly anticipated the course of future change it is not their assumptions about the reliability of these trends as indicators that has misled them.)

It is true that Marx does refer to a number of trends which seemed to him to be implicit in the development of capitalist society, and that some of these trends did *not* continue into modern times—for instance, the tendency of capital to become concentrated in fewer and fewer hands, and the tendency for the bourgeoisie and the proletariat to absorb other social classes and to become increasingly polarized. It would be misleading, though, to suggest that Marx's mistake was simply to observe the trends and to conclude erroneously that they were actually laws. What he was actually trying to do was to look behind such trends in an attempt to find the economic mechanisms which were responsible for them. Popper concedes, in fact, that Marx did have some predictive successes, but argues that "it was nowhere his historicist method which led him to success, but always the methods of institutional analysis."[3] Unfortunately, it seems to be the case that it was his methods of institutional analysis which also produced Marx's failures rather than some distinctive "historicist method," and it may well be there that we have to hunt for the flaws in his prognoses.

Science fiction writers, like human scientists, also pay a lot of attention to trends. Indeed, it is they rather than the social theorists whose main interest in trends lies in their extrapolation rather than in discovering the logic which underlies them. There are many SF stories which do produce images of the future simply by extrapolating trends. It is obvious, though, that most SF writers do not extrapolate trends naïvely, and they know full well that when they do so they are *not* in the business of prophesying. John W. Campbell's introduction to Groff Conklin's classic anthology *The Best of Science Fiction* (1946) explains quite clearly and explicitly why this method cannot be prophetic, and might be regarded as one of the important apologies for the poverty of science-fictional prophecy.

OPENING MINDS, BY BRIAN STABLEFORD

Science fiction writers who play the game of "If This Goes On..." (an early novella by Robert Heinlein used this as a title) are usually very conscious of the implications of the *If*. Stories of this type are often satirical, making the point that trends are subject to *extrapolatio ad absurdum*. Some Malthusian SF stories fit into this category—Kurt Vonnegut's "Tomorrow and Tomorrow and Tomorrow," for instance. Nonsatirical stories of trend-extrapolation are frequently alarmist—this category, too, includes Malthusian fantasies like John Brunner's *Stand on Zanzibar* and Robert Silverberg's *The World Inside*—and can best be understood as imaginative propaganda for "moral restraint." These stories "fail" as prophecies (they are not, of course, intended as such) because they do extrapolate trends further than is warranted, but it does not follow at all that the general failure of science-fictional images of the future has the same cause. Indeed, the evidence surely is that SF writers do not invest much faith in trend-extrapolation as a means of prediction.

In fairness to Popper, it must be admitted that human scientists and SF writers alike are often inclined to be pessimistic about the prospects of trend-breaking. Malthus made room in his theory for moral restraint, but he was obviously sceptical about the probability of our ever managing to control the increase of population in such a careful and calculated way. Alarmist science fiction often has the same pessimistic edge to it.

One of Popper's chief arguments against Marx, therefore (and one of his main reasons for disapproving of Marxism), is that Marx does not reckon much to moral restraint as a force in human affairs. Popper begins his description of Marx's method by emphasizing its deterministic character, and quotes the famous passage from the introduction to *Kapital* where Marx alleges that even a society which has discovered the laws underlying history cannot "overleap the natural phases of its evolution" into a new era but can only "shorten and lessen its birth-pangs."[4] Marx and Engels, indeed, were always at pains to emphasize the difference between their "scientific socialism" and the "Utopian socialism" of other writers, which seemed naïvely to presuppose that a new era could be ushered in simply by political consensus.[5]

It is this fundamental determinism which, according to Popper, leads Marx to confuse trends and laws, and we must consider seriously whether it is here that the real fault lies. It is possible that Marx's anticipations failed simply because he did not realize the extent to which the shape of the future would be determined by the idiosyncratic choices of human beings, which are unpredictable simply because people can do as they like. Certainly, some apologists for the poverty of science-fictional prophecy have made their case on these grounds; an example is the introductory chapter of G. K. Chesterton's *The Napoleon of Notting Hill*, where the fact that the future will always "Cheat the Prophet" is credited simply to human perversity.

Marxism, SF, and the Poverty of Prophecy

We often hear this kind of argument offered as "common sense," where it appears to be widely believed that humans are innately perverse, irrational, and unpredictable. Popper, though, does not labor this point, and his criticism of Marx's pessimism about the power of men to remake their destiny is cautious. Popper knows full well that the choices which people make are at least partly determined by their social circumstances, and that matters of collective decision are often severely limited. Chesterton knew this too, though he regretted it, which is why his tongue was in his cheek when he wrote the first chapter of *The Napoleon of Notting Hill* (not to mention the rest of it). Few human scientists have ever endorsed the view that human behavior is innately irrational and unpredictable to more than a small degree—we need only recall Mill's argument that we all believe that when we know our friends well we know how they will react in different circumstances, or Spencer's observation that we need not deny free will in order to predict that a man in the path of a runaway carriage will avoid it if he can, to be persuaded of the fact ourselves. It is, of course, an important part of the human-scientific enterprise to attempt to explain *why* people make the kinds of choices they habitually do, and how this affects collective decision-making; no one seriously disputes that it does make sense to ask such questions and seek such explanations.

It is true that Marx is overly deterministic in his thinking at certain key points in his theory. Most modern Marxists concede the point, and Marx's own later writings come to the very brink of surrender. The realm of politics is not quite so tightly constrained by the relations of production in the "economic base" of society as Marx sometimes alleged. The question still remains, though, of whether it is *this* flaw in his theory which is responsible for its failure to generate correct anticipations. Certainly it has something to do with it, but it is not the whole of the story and this is not a sensible place to stop the argument. If Marx's "scientific socialism" failed to produce accurate images of the future, so did the Utopian socialism from which he dissented. It is not enough to say that the future is undetermined because we can shape it with our political decisions; we still need to ask why we cannot anticipate what those decisions and their effects are likely to be. If we really did live in the kind of world described in *The Napoleon of Notting Hill*, where an amiably perverse eccentric could be awarded dictatorial power by lottery, then we could simply give up on the project of anticipating the future, but we do not. Because we do not, we cannot give up either on the project of trying to explain why those anticipations always fail.

Science fiction writers, as we have noted, tend to agree with human scientists that human behavior is not entirely irrational or unpredictable. They are often prepared to take an interest in the ways in which people's perceptions, ideas, and behavior are affected by their social circumstances. There is a considerable body of contemporary SF whose explicit purpose is to dramatize this point, by trying to imagine the thoughts and actions of people who find themselves in strange (sometimes bizarre) social milieux. One of the enduring themes of modern SF is the difficulty of making a "conceptual breakthrough" which will allow an individual to transcend the limits of his or her artificial horizons. Examples of this type of story include Clifford D. Simak's "Target Generation," Wyman Guin's "Beyond Bedlam," and James Blish's "Surface Tension."

It seems, therefore, that there is a degree of consensus here between all parties, to the effect that the realm of human choice *is* confined and constrained in certain important ways, which makes radical breaks in history very difficult to achieve. This implies very strongly that we must not shrug off the question of why it is impossible to predict the future simply by invoking the freedom of the will. Of course, we will not get anywhere by *denying* the freedom of people to make choices, but no one in fact does this. For all his pessimism about our inability to overleap the "natural phases" in social development, Marx clearly saw himself as a man who had achieved a "conceptual breakthrough," and felt that he might help others to do likewise in cultivating a proletarian class-consciousness, thus empowering them to become the midwives of the revolutionary birth of the new era.

In a preface which he added to *The Poverty of Historicism* (1957), Popper offered a further argument relating to the impossibility of prediction, which supplements his main case about there being no laws of succession. This argument suggests that the course of history is "strongly influenced" by the growth of knowledge, and that it would be paradoxical to assert that we can have any knowledge of the future growth of this knowledge (how can we know today what we will not discover until tomorrow?).[6]

With reference to both Marx and science fiction, this is perhaps the most interesting of all the arguments about the poverty of prophecy, because it is in relation to this point that there arises the sharpest contrast between Marx's anticipation and the futuristic imagery of SF.

The growth of knowledge has a peculiar place in Marxist thought. There is very little attention paid in Marx's own writings to the advancement of scientific theory, and some of his modern adherents have been sceptical of such theory, considering it to be corrupted to some degree by bourgeois ideology. Jürgen Habermas and others have suggested that some of what passes for an objective description of the natural world is really a disguised attempt to justify aspects of capitalist exploitation, while the Soviet establishment's long-standing suspicion of Darwinian evolutionary theory and Einsteinian relativity theory is well-known. On the other hand, Marx pays a great deal of attention to the historical development of means of production—including technological means. He says hardly anything about the relationship between theory and technology, but his materialist perspective and his suspicion of those theorists of history (Feuerbach, for instance) who give primacy to the history of ideas certainly suggest that he does not see the growth of technology as something generated by or dependent upon the advancement of theory.

Technology plays a strangely ambivalent role in Marx's theory. When he writes about the past, about the succession of economic systems which preceded and led to capitalism, he frequently refers to changes in "the forces of production" as explanatory factors. At times, as in the famous passage from *The Poverty of Philosophy* where he observes that "the windmill gives you society with the feudal lord; the steam mill, society with the industrial capitalist,"[7] he appears to endorse technological determinism—the thesis that social change consists of a series of institutional adaptations to the growth of technological resources. Contemporary opinion is divided as to whether Marx really was a technological determinist—W. H. Shaw argues that he was,[8] while Angus Walker says that it would be absurd to consider him as such,[9] but there is no need to argue the point. One thing that is certain is that when he speaks about likely future developments of the capitalist system he says nothing at all about the possible impact of new technologies. More machines may increase the proportion of constant capital involved in the production process,[10] and hence help to increase the exploitation of the workers by squeezing profits, but new technological discoveries cannot, in Marx's view, make any real difference to the basic situation of developing class conflict. The coming revolution will be an all-out war between the contending classes, not a new Industrial Revolution.

Science fiction writers have typically taken a very different view of the relationship between theory and technology, and of the role which new technologies play in social change. They usually work from assumptions diametrically opposed to those of Marx. For Marx, the role played by machinery in productive processes is a subsidiary one, because in the labor theory of value which he espoused machinery cannot add value—a machine used by a worker is simply putting back into a production process the labor invested in its own making.[11] For SF writers, by contrast, machines are spectacular sources of value, conjuring up huge increases in productive power. Science fiction writers have always been fascinated by the idea that single inspirational discoveries have the power to transform the energy-economy of the world more-or-less at a stroke. The role played by the idea of atomic power in much early SF provides the cardinal example of this kind of thinking. New structural materials and manufacturing processes tend to be represented in SF as liberating forces which sometimes take human labor-power out of the productive process altogether.

There is, of course, some historical significance in this dramatic difference of perspective. Marx died in 1883; his major works were produced between 1844 (the *Economic and Philosophical Manu-*

scripts) and 1867 (*Kapital*, Vol. I), and reflect an era dominated by the clumsy gargantuan steam engines which drove mill-machinery and locomotives. It was still possible for a man whose idea of machinery was based on such cast-iron dinosaurs to hold to the belief that a working machine could only redeem the labor-power invested in its making before it wore out. The idea of machinery typical of science fiction was as yet unborn (and this shows up clearly in the futuristic fictions of the period—see Darko Suvin's comprehensive bibliography of *Victorian Science Fiction in the UK*). It was not until a new phase of the Industrial Revolution began with the multifarious applications of electrical power that ideas about the role and potential of machinery were forced to change. It is no coincidence that Thomas Alva Edison, the prolific inventor of electrical gadgets, was an important hero-figure in early American SF.

Thus, we find that even in SF stories which are closely based in Marxian *political* ideas—for instance, "Through the Horn or the Ivory Gate" in Anatole France's *The White Stone,* Ignatius Donnelly's *Caesar's Column*, and Claude Farrère's *Useless Hands*—we find machinery playing a conspicuously different role from that allotted to it in *Kapital*. It is highly significant that *The White Stone*—which includes the most thoughtful and sensitive attempt ever made to imagine and describe a Marxian communist society—is really a book about the poverty of prophecy. Anatole France already knew, in 1905, that the futuristic dimension in Marx's thought was crooked.

It could be convincingly argued, given all this, that it was his folly in holding to the labor theory of value—especially insofar as it related to the role played by machinery in productive processes—that led Marx to his mistaken prognoses regarding the future development of capitalism. Certainly, some modern economists, contemplating the things that have happened instead of the polarization of the bourgeoisie and the proletariat and their consequent mutual ruination, have used explanations which are heavily dependent on the role of technology: the cardinal example is John Kenneth Galbraith's analysis of "the imperatives of technology" in *The New Industrial State*. If we are to take this argument seriously, then it does seem that Marx fell into the trap described in Popper's preface to *The Poverty of Historicism*: he failed to anticipate the future evolution of capitalism because he failed to anticipate the future developments in scientific knowledge which generated the technology which transformed production processes and social relations of production.

Unfortunately, if we refer back to science fiction we will see that there is something odd about Popper's argument, which casts doubt on the contention that this really is the heart of the matter.

What Popper says is, of course, true. We cannot predict future discoveries in scientific theory. But scientific theory does not affect society *directly*—it does so most importantly by its effect on the growth

Marxism, SF, and the Poverty of Prophecy

of our technological resources. It is the machines we develop which are the powerful agents of social change (and we need not embrace technological determinism in order to accept this), not the theories themselves. Science fiction writers have never been able to anticipate future developments in scientific theory, but this has not prevented their being able to anticipate—often quite cleverly—the new kinds of machines that might become available by courtesy of such developments. Thus, as we have observed, ignorance of the actual theory involved did not prevent early SF writers from imagining atomic power, and SF writers did not need to wait for the invention of the silicon chip to start them thinking about the potential uses of sophisticated computers.

The great majority of SF stories deal with imaginary technologies that are radically different from ones which subsequently developed in actuality (to date, at least). There is, however, a substantial minority of stories which *do* deal with technological innovations that have been realized. There is a sense in which these stories are dodging Popper's prophet-trap—while not anticipating what we will know tomorrow, they are anticipating what that knowledge might allow us to *do*.

It is these stories which are sometimes held up as shining examples of the prophetic power of science fiction: atom bomb stories like Harold Nicolson's *Public Faces* or Cleve Cartmill's "Deadline"; innumerable stories in which rocket-ships carry men for the first time to the surface of the moon. If we look at such stories, though, it is easy to see that their prophetic power does not extend much, if at all, beyond the actual gadgets themselves. Early stories of atomic power, from Wells's *The World Set Free* to John W. Campbell Jr.'s "Blindness," can hardly be said to have produced an accurate account of the social consequences of the realization of atomic chain reactions. Where science-fictional prophecies fall down, even when they are right about future gadgets, is in calculations about how society will be affected by them. It is not future technology which SF writers cannot anticipate; it is what Galbraith calls "the imperatives of technology."

This may mean only that SF writers are incompetent, and that if they only had the analytical flair of a Galbraith (or a Marx) they could have produced much more sensible images of the 1990s in the 1930s. On the other hand, it might signify that there still remains something important to notice about the poverty of prophecy. It seems to be the case that the two Popperian arguments so far described do suffice to explain the poverty of Marx's anticipations (though it may be the one Popper discovered later rather than the one he uses in *The Open Society and Its Enemies* that turns the trick), but it still may make sense to be suspicious of them as *general* explanations of the poverty of prophecy.

There is in *The Poverty of Historicism* another observation about the difficulty of prediction, which is discovered in the early pages,[12] but which then drops out of sight for the remainder of the argument. This is a pity, because it is an interesting point, and one which is capable of confusing the whole issue quite considerably. This is the "Oedipus effect," which refers to the influence which a prediction can have upon the predicted event.

The reference to the myth of Oedipus here recalls the fact that Oedipus was abandoned to die by his father because a prophecy was made that Oedipus would one day become his father's murderer. Unfortunately, the abandonment of the child set in train a chain of events which led eventually to the murder. One kind of Oedipus effect, therefore, is the self-fulfilling prophecy, of which the best-known example is the anthropological anecdote about the witch-doctor who can instill fatal despair in his victim simply by informing him that he will die. Popper also observes that there are self-negating prophecies too. A simple example would be provided by a person who consults an astrologer about the prospects of an enterprise, and on hearing that it is doomed to disaster, alleviates the very possibility of disaster by doing something else instead.

Popper does not appear to think that the Oedipus effect has much bearing on social science, but he does mention it briefly in *The Open Society and Its Enemies*. The only mention of it in connection with Marx[13] suggests that even if Marx's prophecies had come true, they would not have proved his theory correct, because they might have been self-fulfilling prophecies. Popper clearly does not realize the significance of conceding this, because the other side of the same argumentative coin is surely that the fact that Marx's prophecies have *not* come true therefore cannot suffice to prove his theory false, because they might have been self-negating prophecies. It is not surprising that Popper does not make this comment, given the vital importance played in his philosophy of science by the falsification of predictions. If falsification lost its significance in respect of human science, then Popper's ambition to provide a single all-inclusive logic of scientific method would begin to look a bit sick.

Perhaps we should be prepared to give some consideration, though, to the possibility that Marx's anticipations failed to materialize because insofar as they functioned as prophecies they actually worked to negate themselves. If Marx failed to supply the proletariat with the conceptual breakthrough which would equip them with revolutionary class-consciousness, perhaps he had better luck with the bourgeoisie. Perhaps it was *they* who were sufficiently impressed and inspired by his analysis to act in just such a way as to prevent his prognoses from being realized. After all, as the *Communist Manifesto* reminds us, the working men of the world had nothing to lose but their chains; the bourgeois capitalists had *everything* to lose, and thus every incentive to make sure that it could not be taken away from them by inexorable developments in the logic of the situation. As soon as they found out that the logic of the situation even permitted the possibility that "the expropriators

MARXISM, SF, AND THE POVERTY OF PROPHECY

[could be] expropriated,"14 they were surely motivated to alter the situation and subvert its logic. In all probability, the nineteenth-century capitalists did not need to read Marx in order to come to this conclusion; despite the alleged mystifications of their ideology, they were surely able to see something of the logic of their situation by themselves.

This possibility adds a whole new dimension to our consideration of the poverty of prophecy. We have seen that Marx did fail to take proper account of the future growth of knowledge and its significance in altering—through the medium of new technologies—the social relations of production. Perhaps, though, this was not his only failure, nor even his most vital failure, when he tried to anticipate the course of future history. He also did not take into account the way in which the understanding which men have of a situation and its likely development (whether that understanding be correct or not) can affect their handling of the situation. Thus, for instance, men armed with Marxist ideas might act very differently from those who had not made the same conceptual breakthrough—something that certainly seems to have played a significant part in human political affairs ever since the Russian revolution of October 1917.

If we turn back again to science fiction, it may seem hard to believe that the Oedipus effect could possibly have a bearing on the failure of SF as prophecy, for the simple reason that no one takes SF stories seriously enough for them to be self-fulfilling or self-negating. However, at least some SF stories have been conspicuously successful in providing powerful images that seem now to play a leading part in our thinking about the future. Two novels—*Brave New World* and *Nineteen Eighty-Four*—have been especially important in this regard. It is true that no one seriously thinks that particular SF stories accurately portray the future, but when we *do* try to imagine what the future may hold for us, the ideas of science fiction (and not just the gadgets) do provide us with an important resource.

The images of future society in SF are not *believed*, but they do not have to be believed in order to be taken seriously as warnings or reassurances. They do not tell us where our discoveries will lead us, but we can still take some of them seriously as arguments about where discoveries *might* be able to take us. The poverty of their prophecy thus might consist in empowering us to avoid the more frightening of their possible futures. (There is thus a curious sense in which, if science-fictional prophecies of nuclear holocaust are to prove poverty-stricken, the stories will have succeeded as warnings in failing as prophecies.)

It will be clear now why this last argument about the poverty of prophecy confuses the whole issue rather than simply offering one more reason why prophets never get it right. It calls into question what we can and do mean by "getting it right." It is conceivable—though it is difficult to be sure—that the history of human science has been cursed by the Oedipus effect. The history of economics, for instance, can easily be seen from this perspective as an ironic story of theories which, as soon as they begin to cast light on a situation, empower people to act in such a way that the situation promptly changes, and has to be interpreted all over again. It is possible too that the real utility of clever anticipations of the future (whether in human science or in fiction) has nothing to do with the likelihood of their coming true, and everything to do with their power to affect the choices and collective decisions that people make.

If this is so, then the poverty of prophecy might, after all, be its virtue and not its sin.

IX.

FUTURE WARS, 1890-1950

This essay attempts to investigate the complex relationship between the actual pattern of history and a particular tradition in speculative fiction that developed alongside it. In attempting to anticipate possible futures, speculative fiction constantly accomodates itself to each actual turn of events, changing its estimates of probability and possibility, and thus changing its evaluations of contemporary men and their actions. It is this process of sporadic reaction and re-evaluation which guides the evolution of speculative fiction, and the process can be seen with particular clarity in connection with the present subject-matter.

In looking at images of imaginary warfare this essay is an extension of a study begun by one of the most interesting and important books on imaginative fiction: I. F. Clarke's *Voices Prophesying War 1763-1984*. To some extent, it is a mere amplification of arguments and observations already found in Clarke's book, but its separate existence is justified in two ways. On the one hand, it will pay closer attention to a period which is covered rather superficially in Clarke: the era between the two world wars. On the other hand, in focussing quite narrowly on the impact on imaginative fiction of the experience of the Great War, it will hopefully provide a warrant for some original comments on the relationship between images of future war and the social situations which generate them.

I. F. Clarke has described in detail the origins of the British future war story and the crucial influence of George Chesney's novelette, "The Battle of Dorking," first published in 1871. There is no need to reproduce this account even in summary, save to say that "The Battle of Dorking" is a journalistic description of an imaginary battle in which an invading German army has no difficulty in overwhelming the ill-equipped and ill-trained defenders of Britain. The story was a great success, both as a popular literary work and as a piece of political propaganda; it called forth many imitations and established a curious genre of speculative fictions. For the purposes of the present work, though, it is necessary to look more closely at the boom in future war stories which occurred in the 1890s, when the genre was taken up enthusiastically by the popular magazines of the day, as a weapon in their circulation war.

The rapid expansion of the popular magazine market in the 1890s, following the success of *The Strand* (launched in January 1891), created a new world of opportunity for writers of fiction. Most of the new magazines—particularly those at the lower end of the market—published a good deal of fiction, and competed fiercely to find fiction which would attract the attention of new readers. In pursuit of this aim several editors attempted to reproduce the sensational effect produced twenty years earlier by "The Battle of Dorking." In 1892 *Black and White* serialized "The Great War of 1892," a mock-journalistic account by P. H. Colomb and several collaborators of a conflict involving several of the more powerful European nations. It was reprinted in book form the following year as *The Great War of 189-*. Also in 1892 A. N. Seaforth published *The Last Great Naval War*, and *The Engineer* serialized "The Captain of the *Mary Rose*" by W. Laird Clowes. All three works concentrated on the art and science of naval warfare, and all three attempted to be carefully realistic in their estimates of the way that a new war might be fought.

As things turned out, however, faithful adherence to the documentary style was not the strategy which attracted the largest readership. The greatest success among these new future war fantasies was serialized in 1893 in *Pearson's Weekly*, having been commissioned by the publisher from one of his hack journalists, George Griffith. This was *The Angel of the Revolution*, in which the next war is fought not with ironclad ships and field guns, but with airships, submarines, and bombs of awesome explosive power. Redolent with descriptions of bombed cities and the mass slaughter of civilians, this novel cut casually across the assumptions made by expert prognosticators. According to Griffith, the kind of war featured in *The Great War of 189-* was already obsolete, because science was about to arm men with such powerful instruments of war that the whole nature of international conflict must be transformed.

The heroes of *The Angel of the Revolution* are self-styled Terrorists who make war on tyrants and political systems in the name of the oppressed peoples of the world; theirs is not merely one more in an endless series of petty squabbles between nations, but a war to settle the future of mankind: a world war and a war to end war. It ends with a climactic confrontation between the Terrorists (who have already triumphed in the West) and the hordes of Islam:

> The war-balloons moved slowly forward in a straight line at an elevation of four thousand feet, sweeping the Moslem host from van to rear with a ceaseless hail of melinite and cyanogen bombs. Great projectiles soared silently up from the water to the

north, and where they fell buildings were torn to fragments, great holes were blasted into the earth, and every human being within the radius of the explosion was blown to pieces, or hurled stunned to the ground. But more mysterious and terrible than all were the effects of the assault delivered by the air-ships, which divided into squadrons and swept hither and thither in wide curves, with the sunlight shining on their silvery hulls and their long slender guns, smokeless and flameless, hurling the most awful missiles of all far and wide, over a scene of butchery and horror that beggared all description.

In vain the gallant Moslems looked for enemies in the flesh to confront them. None appeared save a few sentinels across the Bosphorus. And still the work of slaughter went on, pitiless and passionless as the earthquake or the thunderstorm. Millions of shots were fired into the air without result, and by the time the rain of death had been falling without intermission for two hours, an irresistible panic fell upon the Moslem soldiery. They had never met enemies like these before, and, brave as lions and yet simple as children, they looked upon them as something more than human, and with one accord they flung away their weapons and raised their hands in supplication to the sky. Instantly the aerial bombardment ceased, and within an hour East and West had shaken hands...and the long warfare of Cross and Crescent had ceased, as men hoped, for ever.[1]

Although the pressure of commercial priorities persuaded Griffith to provide a sequel to the novel, *The Angel of the Revolution* is an account of the climacticon in human affairs: an apocalypse not merely due, but to be welcomed. He was well enough aware that a conflict such as he described must involve the deaths of millions of people, with little distinction to be drawn between soldiers and civilians, but considered this as merely part of the price to be paid for entry into a new and better era. Griffith saw the next war as a kind of *rite de passage* for mankind. The sequel, *Olga Romanoff*, simply plays the whole drama through again, in more sensational fashion, to a similar conclusion when the Terrorists survive to repopulate the world after a cosmic disaster.

Other contemporary writers clearly considered that Griffith had gone over the top in his lurid presentation of the shape of the war to come, but most moved quickly enough to a position of compromise. William Le Queux, called upon to provide the first of his many future war novels in order to enable the rival magazine *Answers to Correspondents* to reply to *Pearson's* in kind, offered "The Poisoned Bullet" (1893; reprinted in book form as *The Great War in England in 1897*). Le Queux returned to the tried-and-true formula of an invasion of England, but was ready enough to raise the stakes in terms of casualty figures and images of wholesale slaughter. E. Douglas Fawcett, in a work blatantly imitative of Griffith, *Hartmann the Anarchist* (1893), was willing to accept airships as a new weapon of war, but was careful to dissent from the extremes of Griffith's politics, drawing a sharp distinction between the evil terrorist Hartmann and the good socialists who are more careful and gentle in their plans for world reform. (Griffith apparently took Fawcett's point, and made a similar distinction in his own novel, *The Outlaws of the Air*, in 1895.)

When *The Captain of the Mary Rose*, *The Angel of the Revolution*, and *Hartmann the Anarchist* appeared in book form they were all illustrated by Fred T. Jane, already famous as a naval illustrator (he is commemorated even today in *Jane's Fighting Ships*, *Jane's Fighting Aircraft*, and other such guides, which have been published in uninterrupted series from his beginnings). Jane produced a very sober and conservative future war novel of his own in *Blake of the Rattlesnake* (1895), but even this was about submarine warfare, and he went on to write other scientific romances which clearly showed how Griffith's imaginative extravagance had infected him.

As the years went by, Griffith's ideas began to recur more frequently and more obviously. The notion of a war to end war became popular, often in association with some kind of social Darwinist thinking which imagined that there was a crucial issue to be settled once and for all between the races of man. Louis Tracy, who worked, like Griffith, for C. Arthur Pearson, wrote a fervently militaristic account of *The Final War* (1896), in which the British Empire survives an evil conspiracy of European powers to establish Anglo-Saxon hegemony for all time. The last chapter of the novel is a virtual sermon:

> For the message which Science gave the world was that that race alone would conquer in the struggle for existence which showed greatest adaptability, which could easiest accomodate itself to the countless variations of earth's wayward moods. It was the cruel law of the survival of the fittest. There was need of some versatile people who feared no change of climate or contradiction of condition, for whom heat and cold, desert and fertile land, sea and plain, peace and war, luxury and indigence, struggle and ease were alike—whose temperament had infinite degrees passing from sanguine heat to phlegmatic torpor. For

such a race the earth lay open, offering its dominion....

This, then, is the mission of the Saxon race—slowly but surely to pour itself over the earth, to absorb the nations, to bring to pass that wonderful dream of a world united in a single family and speaking a common speech.2

Tracy suggested to his friend M. P. Shiel that he also should write a story of this kind, and Shiel produced "The Empress of the Earth" (1898; reprinted in book form as *The Yellow Danger*) for another Pearson publication, *Short Stories*. Here the war is between the white and yellow races, to determine which will inherit the earth. Most of the conflict is orthodox, with elaborate descriptions of naval engagements, but in a quasi-apocalyptic finale the oriental invaders of mainland Europe are destroyed by means of bacteriological warfare. The ending of the novel echoes Tracy's ("The sceptre of Britain, therefore, stretched from pole to pole, and from the river to the ends of the earth"), but with a cautionary note ("If the world is to become English, the English must first become worldly"). As to how the world may be unified, Shiel merely notes that the invention of the airship must be imminent, and that its advent must change completely the relations between men, shrinking the world and paving the way for a common culture.

The jingoism of these novels is something uniquely British, but the myth of a war to end war can also be found in the few American future war novels of this period, including *The Great War Syndicate* (1889) by Frank R. Stockton, and *Armageddon* (1898) by Stanley Waterloo. The latter is somewhat extravagantly titled, in that it describes a limited naval engagement in which a single flying machine plays a crucial role, but there is much discussion weighing the races of the world in the balance, and its conclusion is uncompromising in pointing the way to the future:

> Civilization has reached a point where war is suicide. When one hundred thousand men meet another one hundred thousand men and the only possible sequence of their meeting means that one hundred thousand of the two hundred thousand men must be slain, there isn't going to be any fighting...Never in any battle fought in all the history of the world have the bravest of all the men of the world faced such dreadful chance. They could not unless they were fools....
>
> The time of powder and ball has gone by. In war, already, tons of high explosives are hurled, and every mechanical device of man in his greatest devel-

opment of control over nature is employed in this manner to destroy human lives. When aerial warfare is added, the end will have come...There can be no safety for anyone, and the heads of nations will hesitate before they declare war....

The menace of fatal war must preserve alive, as it has heretofore, many a nation, and keep it in peace. To have a world at peace there must be massed in the controlling nations such power of destruction as may not even be questioned. So we shall build our appliances of destruction, calling to our aid every discovery and achievement of science. When there are but chances about war, when it means death to all, or the vast majority of all who engage in it, there will be peace.[3]

The confident assertion made in the first quoted paragraph would have sounded appallingly hollow had it been related to the armies which clashed again and again upon the Somme, and the naive statement of the logic of deterrents can hardly seem convincing today, but in the closing years of the nineteenth century this seemed a plausible viewpoint.

The man who really tried hard to achieve a sensible compromise between Griffith's conviction that technology would profoundly alter the business of war and the more conservative viewpoint which held that imminent apocalypse was hardly to be anticipated was H. G. Wells. In his classic early work of futurological analysis, *Anticipations* (1901), he took pains to consider carefully the possible effects of technological advancement on the conduct of war, and came up with a description of near-future warfare remarkably like the kind of trench warfare that actually was to dominate the Great War. He foresaw the roles played by observation balloons, heavy artillery, light machine guns, and even by pestilence. Aeroplanes, interestingly, play little part in this scenario (although Wells had already described an aerial battle in his novel, *When the Sleeper Wakes*, in 1899), and he confessed himself quite unable to imagine submarines fulfilling any useful function. Two years later, in his short story, "The Land Ironclads," he incorporated the tank into his notion of future warfare, but then the Wright brothers took to the air, and he was moved to revise his estimate entirely.

In *The War in the Air* (1908) Wells produced a radically new interpretation of the significance of new technology in the business of war. Here, aerial bombing quickly secures the destruction of civilization. Although the first chapter includes a wry acknowledgment of the unexpected foresight of George Griffith, the story moves inexorably to a conclusion very much more pessimistic than that of *The Angel of the Revolution*. This is a war to end war, certainly, but the sole reason for the end of war is the obliteration of the ability to *make* war: the world is bombed back to a new Dark Age, all the gains of social evolution lost as the delicately balanced web of social relationships collapses. Each community must learn to be self-sufficient again, rediscovering basic survival skills which the division of labor and specialization of endeavor had long made irrelevant.

If the essay in *Anticipations* showed remarkable foresight in approximating more closely than any other vision the real form of the Great War, *The War in the Air* was equally remarkable in approximating most closely the form of the future war stories which followed the Great War. It is significant, though, that Wells moved again from this position before the war actually broke out. In *The World Set Free* (1914), published on the very eve of the Great War, he had already begun considering a war fought with atomic bombs. Here, though, the destruction of civilization is not altogether disastrous; rather, the awesome power of the new bombs quickly brings home the lesson that man can no longer afford to go to war. The ruination of the old world is here a necessary prelude to the building of a new one, where old enmities are set aside and a new era of social justice is begun. The peaceful uses of atomic power, once the bombs have been put away, secure the future happiness and prosperity of the world. Thus, Wells retreated into the camp of Griffith and Stanley Waterloo.

Griffith, though he wrote many other future war stories after *Olga Romanoff*, never produced anything else as impressive as *The Angel of the Revolution*. His work degenerated into tired self-plagiarism, but he remained loyal to his own mythology. His last novel, *The Lord of Labor* (1911), was not published until five years after his death in 1906, but was still comfortably ahead of technological developments in the real world. It imagines the next war being fought with atomic missiles and disintegrator rays. The notion of a crucial transformation of human affairs is not invoked here, but M. P. Shiel did not hesitate to repeat himself in that regard when he revisited the imaginative territory of *The Yellow Danger* in *The Dragon* (1913; later revised as *The Yellow Peril*).

Other writers, by contrast, remained cynical about a war to end war. The authentic tradition of "The Battle of Dorking" was sustained by numerous books which provided support for the political cause of the redoubtable Lord Roberts, who continually agitated for more spending on armaments and railed against Britain's unpreparedness for war. One of the great successes of the early years of the twentieth century was William Le Queux's *The Invasion of 1910* (1906), which helped to boost the circulation of Alfred Harmsworth's *Daily Mail*. There were a great many novels which ignored altogether the issue of new weapons and new modes of fighting, but were content to play upon the fear of invasion. There were several notable stories of "aborted wars" where plans to invade England are found out in advance and thwarted, including Max Pemberton's *Pro Patria* (1901) and Erskine Childers's classic, *The Riddle of the Sands* (1903). There were also novels where England has to suffer the awful ignominy of defeat and occupation in order to realize how frightfully her people have betrayed their nation; examples include A. J. Dawson's *The Message* (1907) and the brilliant *When William Came* by Saki (H. H. Munro).

There seems little doubt that these latter kinds of novel were in better tune with the spirit of the time. Wells and Griffith were regarded as essentially fanciful writers—purveyors of sensational scientific romance—and most people had no difficulty in holding the products of their imagination at some distance. If the mythology of a war to end war became popular, it was not really in the sense that Griffith and Wells used the notion, but rather in a much narrower sense, more to do with teaching the would-be German imperialists not to be so bellicose.

That *The War in the Air* cannot have been taken too seriously as an anti-war polemic is clearly indicated by the response to two infinitely milder exercises in propaganda, both published in the months before the war began. *War* by W. Douglas Newton is an impassioned plea for the avoidance of war, and carries a supposedly provocative preface by Robert Hugh Benson warning that the horrors it describes could actually come to pass. The book was virtually ignored, and did not warrant reprinting; there is an ironic humor to be found today in comparing the wilder excesses of Newton's imaginings with the events of the real war. Newton attempts to shock his readers by suggesting such frightful things as the allegation that in such a war medical teams might favor the injured on their own side and neglect others, that women might be raped by soldiers, and that civilians might be shot for resisting the demands of invading armies. These really were the horizons of the popular imagination. In "Danger!," a novelette written for *The Strand*, Sir Arthur Conan Doyle suggested that in the event of war England would be dangerously vulnerable because enemy submarines would prevent supply ships from getting through. This called forth dismissive denials from the Admiralty, who were convinced that no enemy could possibly behave in such an unsportsmanlike way if it involved attacking noncombatants. Within a hundred days the first merchant ships had been sent to the bottom, and the Germans were trying to build a U-boat blockade around the British Isles.

The pattern of ideas reflected in future war stories published before the Great War, therefore, is a confused one. The extent to which the pattern reflected an actual distribution of attitudes within the population is, of course, very difficult to estimate, but the probability is that those stories which hindsight exposes to us as the most prophetic would have been regarded as extravagant fantasies. Whatever anxieties there were in pre-1914 Britain about the possibly disastrous nature of a new war did not run particularly deep. Even those people who could imagine disaster tended to fall back on an argument which transformed catastrophe into a kind of social rebirth.

What contribution the profusion of future war stories made to the readiness of Britons to fight the Great War is impossible to estimate. Certainly, it was widely believed that the war was necessary and inevitable. For nearly two generations there had been political pressure groups demanding reform of the army and the replacement of obsolescent weaponry, and these pressure groups put their stamp on a great deal of the future war fiction that was produced. (Lord Roberts appears as a character in many such novels, including ones by Griffith, Tracy, and Le Queux.)

The real Great War was not the kind of affair imagined in *The Invasion of 1910* or in Newton's *War*, but something very much more horrible. It was certainly not a war to end war, nor a war to pave the way for the salvaging of civilization. (Even in 1918, though, there were optimistic fantasies being produced to envisage the Utopian reconstruction of Britain after the war; examples are *The New Moon* by Oliver Onions and *The Tower* by "Watchman.") It did not bring about the destruction of civilization either, but it did provide adequate fuel for the imagination of those who began to speculate about the course of the *next* war.

One of the most widely-read scientific romances of the postwar years was *The People of the Ruins* (1920) by Edward Shanks. It was an influential book, and set an example for several other writers who were disposed to follow in its tracks. In the story, a new war begins in 1924, but the protagonist sees only the beginning of the bombing of London. He is trapped in a bombed building and exposed to a preservative gas which holds him in the thrall of suspended animation for a hundred fifty years. When he awakes, it is to find England in the grip of a new Dark Age akin to that described briefly in the epilogue of *The War in the Air*. Shanks takes up exactly where Wells left off in 1908, but moves in a direction very different from that taken by Wells in *The World Set Free*. Here there is no prospect of renewal.

The hero of *The People of the Ruins* is in a unique position in the new world: he is potentially a storehouse of lost knowledge. In fact, he is ill-fitted for this role, but in the context of this future it hardly matters—all that the rulers of the new world require of him is that he can make the old weapons work again, so that they can continue with their squabbles and secure the decline of man even further into stone age savagery. Even in *The War in the Air* the ending is not totally pessimistic, and the world is at least settled and regretful. The ending of *The People of the Ruins*, by contrast, allows no glimmer of hope:

> Cities would be burnt, bridges broken down, tall towers destroyed and all the wealth and learning of humanity would shiver to a few shards and a little dust. The very place would be forgotten where once had stood the houses that he knew; and the roads he had walked with his friends would be as desolate and lonely as the Stane Street of the Romans.
> Even all this story, his victory and his defeat, his joy and his sorrow, would fade out of the memory of man. But what did it all matter to Jeremy Tuft, who, wonder and portent that he was, strange anachronism, unparallelled and reluctant ambassador from one age to the next, had suffered in the end that common ill, the loss of his beloved? He raised the pistol to his head and fired.[4]

A second version of this same plot appeared in 1922, in *Theodore Savage* by Cicely Hamilton (revised as *Lest Ye Die* in 1928). This more striking work describes the decay of civilization within the lifetime of its eponymous hero. The story begins in the social whirl of London in the 1920s, interrupted by an unexpected war which proceeds according to the logic of "displacement of population"—a theory which involves driving people from the cities by saturation bombing. The displaced population, faced with starvation, quickly falls to internecine fighting, and one bad winter is all that it takes to make England a nation of scattered scavengers. Slowly, communities re-form, but the social order that they adopt is nothing like the one which was shattered; society must be rebuilt from scratch:

> As in every social system from the beginning of time, the community was welded to a conscious whole not by the love its members bore to each other, but by hatred and fear of the outsider; it was the enemy, the urgent common need to be saved from him, that made of man a comrade and a citizen; the peril from outside was the natural antidote to everyday hatreds and the ceaseless bickerings of close neighbours. The instinctive politics of a squalid village were in miniature the policy of vanished nations, and untraditioned little headmen, like dead and gone kings, quelled internal feuds by diverting attention to the danger that threatened from abroad. The foundations of community life in the new world, like the foundations of community life in the old, were laid in the selfishness of fear...the blind, stubborn instincts that created Babylon—created London and Rome and destroyed them—were

laying well and truly in a mud-walled compound the foundations of cities which should rise, flourish, perish in the stead of London and of Rome.5

The return to barbarism is followed inevitably by a return to superstition. The scientific habit of thought disappears with its products, and science becomes the object of a blind fear, stigmatized as that which destroyed the world. Theodore Savage realizes that this may be part of a pattern of eternal recurrence:

> Many times, it might be, since the world began to spin, had men called upon the rocks to cover them from the devils their own hands had fashioned; many times, it might be, a remnant had put from it the knowledge it dared not trust itself to wield—that it might not fall upon its own weapons, but live, just live, like the beasts!6

By means of this inspiration, Savage is able to reinterpret the most ancient myths of his own world, and he stands by as new versions of them are formulated, into which he himself is incorporated once he has become old enough to be mysterious:

> With his death the local legends increased and multiplied; the distorted, varied myths of the Ruin of Man and its causes showing an inevitable tendency to group themselves around one striking and mysterious figure, to make of that figure a cause and a personification of the Great Disaster. Theodore Savage, to those who came after, was Merlin, Frankenstein and Adam; the fool who tasted of forbidden fruit, the magician whose arts had brought ruin on a world, the devil-artisan whose unholy skill had created monsters that destroyed him. His grave was an awesome spot, apart from other graves, which the timorous avoided after dark; and, long after all trace of it had vanished, there clung to the neighbourhood a tradition of haunting and mystery...To his children's children his name was the symbol of a dead civilization; a civilization that had passed so completely from the ken of living man that its lost achievements, the manner of its ending, could only be expressed in symbol.7

The notion of such an eternal cycle of civilizations was not new—it is featured, among other places, in Jules Verne's last work, "The Eternal Adam"—but its incorporation into a story of the near future testifies to a new sense of the fragility of the human world. In the prewar years even cosmic disasters had rarely been credited with the power to obliterate so completely the rewards of social evolution, but the possibility that a new war might comfortably achieve such a devastation was now to be echoed frequently. In John Gloag's *Tomorrow's Yesterday* (1932) it is assumed that man's day is done if he cannot control his warlike impulses, and a new intelligent race evolves from cats to replace us. Gloag is one of several writers whose work in the speculative vein is haunted by the notion of a return to savagery, and it recurs in several of his later stories and novels.

Stories of awesomely destructive wars were produced at regular intervals throughout the twenties and thirties: *The Collapse of Homo Sapiens* (1923) by P. Anderson Graham; *Ragnarok* (1926) by Shaw Desmond; *The Gas War of 1940* (1931) by "Miles" (reissued as *Valiant Clay* by Neil Bell); *The Poison War* (1933) by Ladbroke Black; *The Black Death* (1934) by Moray Dalton.

It is notable that there is little trace of any such anxiety in American science fiction of the same period. The United States had suffered far less from the effects of World War I than any of the European nations, despite the fact that Americans came out of it with a fierce determination not to get caught up in any more European wars. Americans, by and large, could easily evade the suspicion that the end of civilization was at hand. Their fears for the future took different forms. There is little doubt, though, that the kind of anxiety which has its most extreme expression in these fantasies was widely distributed among the British public. The significance of what had been learned from the Great War was not underestimated.

One of the foremost advocates of avoidance of future war was Winston Churchill, who published in *Pall Mall Magazine* in 1924 an article under the provocative title, "Shall We Commit Suicide?" Here he argued that the Great War had ended only just in time, or civilization might already have been destroyed:

> But all that happened in the four years of the Great War was only a prelude to what was preparing for the fifth year. The campaign of the year 1919 would have witnessed an immense accession to the power of destruction. Had the Germans retained the *moral* to make good their retreat to the Rhine, they would have been assaulted in the summer of 1919 with forces and by methods incomparably more prodigious than any yet employed. Thousands of aeroplanes would have shattered their cities. Scores of thousands of cannon would have blasted their front. Arrangements were being made to carry simultaneously a quarter of a million men, together with all

their requirements, continuously forward across country in mechanical vehicles moving ten or fifteen miles each day. Poison gases of incredible malignity, against which only a secret mask (which the Germans could not obtain in time) was proof, would have stifled all resistance and paralyzed all life on the hostile front subjected to attack. No doubt the Germans too had their plans. But the hour of wrath had passed, the signal of relief was given, and the horrors of 1919 remain buried in the archives of the great antagonists.[8]

The article continues:

Certain sombre facts emerge solid, inexorable, like the shapes of mountains from drifting mist. It is established that henceforward whole populations will take part in war, all doing their utmost, all subjected to the fury of the enemy. It is established that nations who believe that their life is at stake will not be restrained from using any means to secure their existence. *It is probable—nay, certain—that among the means which will next time be at their disposal will be agencies and processes of destruction wholesale, unlimited, and, perhaps, once launched, uncontrollable.*[9]

Churchill goes on to talk about chemical warfare, about biological warfare, about bombs which will "concentrate the force of a thousand tons of cordite and blast a township at a stroke," and about flying bombs controlled by radio. Today, of course, it is the superpowerful bombs which have become the primary focus for our anxieties, but in the immediate wake of the Great War the main bugbear was poison gas.

As early as 1907 a pact concerning the use of chemical weapons was made by the signatories of the Hague Peace Conference, but the renunciation extended only to the use of projectiles discharging asphyxiating gases; discharge of gas from cylinders on the ground was not mentioned. During the Great War twenty-five different poison gases were used; the most effective ones were delivered in liquid form to evaporate slowly. Most of the gases were relatively ineffective, but progress was rapid. The one that did most damage was mustard gas, but the most significant development was of a group of poisonous arsenous smokes which were ready for deployment in 1919, but not actually used on any considerable scale. These gases—including the American Lewisite—were the ones referred to by Churchill in the article quoted above. The effects of such smokes are described by J. B. S. Haldane, who worked on the development of chemical weapons during the Great War:

> In small amounts, these smokes merely make one sneeze. In somewhat larger amounts they cause pain of the most terrific character in the head and chest. The pain in the head is described as like that caused when fresh water gets into the nose when bathing, but infinitely more severe. These symptoms are accompanied by the most appalling mental distress and misery. Some soldiers poisoned by these substances had to be prevented from committing suicide; others temporarily went raving mad, and tried to burrow into the ground to escape from imaginary pursuers.[10]

The fact that these new weapons were never widely employed probably added to the apprehension in which they were held. The passage quoted above goes on to note that very few affected soldiers actually died from exposure to the smoke, and that most made a complete recovery within a short period of time; but it was the horrific aspects of the weapon which caught the attention of the public. Then, too, such progress had been made in the development of chemical weapons in a mere four years that it seemed reasonable to expect Lewisite and its kindred to be merely one more station on the road to the most awful and most devastating weapons imaginable.

It is probable that the fear of chemical weapons was greatly exaggerated. Certainly Haldane thought so; the essay which is quoted above is entitled *Callinicus: A Defence of Chemical Warfare* (1925), and argues that chemical weapons are actually more humane than explosives. Haldane points out that not all gases are dangerous to life and health, and that one of the ironies of the Hague Convention was that it permitted the use of mustard gas while banning lachrymatory gases (*i.e.*, tear gases). He argues that chemical warfare *could* concentrate on the business of debilitating enemy soldiers without slaughtering them, and adds that there is surely little moral distinction to be drawn between poisonous gases and swords—if it is right for a man to murder his neighbor with one, how can it be wrong for him to do likewise with the other? At the end of the essay, however, Haldane predicts that no one would listen to his argument, and he was almost right. In all the novels and futurological works that were produced between the wars there is only a bare handful which consider "humane" uses of chemical weapons, or even consider the threat of chemical warfare exaggerated.

By the time Haldane published *Callinicus* an agreement forswearing the use of chemical weapons had been made in Washington in 1922, and soon afterwards this was extended by the Geneva Conference of 1925. It is not surprising, though, that writers of speculative fiction had little confidence in the effectiveness of this ban. Anxiety seems to have been temporarily allayed in the late 1920s, when relatively few future war stories were published, but it certainly began to build again in the 1930s, greatly encouraged by Hitler's rise to power in Germany and by the outbreak of the Spanish Civil War.

On 10 November 1932 Stanley Baldwin made a speech in the House of Commons which reiterated Churchill's insistence on the need to avoid war, recognizing at the same time that there was widespread public anxiety regarding such a possibility:

> What the world suffers from is a sense of fear...a want of confidence....My own view is that there is no one thing that is more responsible for that fear...than the fear of the air....
>
> In the next war you will find that any town within reach of an aerodrome can be bombed within the first five minutes of war to an extent inconceivable in the last war....
>
> I think it is well also for the man in the street to realise that there is no power on earth that can protect him from being bombed, whatever people may tell him. The bomber will always get through.
>
> The only defence is in offence, which means that you have got to kill more women and children more quickly than the enemy, if you want to save yourselves.
>
> ...The prohibition of the bombardment of the civil population...is impracticable so long as any bombardment exists at all....
>
> As far as the air is concerned there is, as has been most truly said, no way of complete disarmament except the abolition of flying. Now that again is impossible.[11]

The presumed threat of air power is widely reflected in stories of the same stripe as "The Battle of Dorking": clarion calls for rearmament and for the reorganization of Britain's military priorities. E. F. Spanner, retired from the Royal Corps of Naval Constructors, wrote and published several novels in the late 1920s arguing for the obsolescence of the British Navy and its helplessness to defend our shores against aerial attack. The novels call for much heavier investment in warplanes, and suggest that if Britain will not commit such investment, her enemies surely will. In *The Broken Trident* (1926) the Germans pay us back for the humiliations heaped on them in consequence of their defeat in the Great War, albeit in a very gentlemanly and sportsmanlike fashion, without so much as a whiff of poison gas. Like "The Battle of Dorking," this novel was quickly translated and published in Germany.

Even the most determindedly realistic pseudo-journalistic accounts of the horrors of modern war work from the premise that lightning bombing raids would follow any declaration of war, and that their effect would be terrible. *Invasion from the Air* (1934) by Frank McIlraith and Roy Connolly, which uses Baldwin's speech as a preface, describes the effects of extensive offensive bombing, involving explosives, incendiary bombs, and already-existent poison gases. Rather than concentrate on the horrors of the mass slaughter, it moves inexorably to the conclusion that the political community of Britain (and of other involved nations) would disintegrate so quickly that by the time the rulers of Europe finally meet to sue for peace not one of them can be sure of hegemony within his own nation. Europe is thus ripe for a Fascist takeover. Similar assumptions are to be found in other novels which put aside the notion of an immediate return to savagery in order to wonder what kind of polity might emerge from the confusion created by a bombing war; Shaw Desmond's *Chaos* (1938) follows a similar course, though the ending dissolves into an empty plea for supernatural redemption which is, if anything, a more eloquent expression of hopelessness than the ruthless pessimism of the likes of Shanks and Hamilton.

It is not surprising that virtually all writers of future war stories in Britain placed such confidence in the efficacy of air raids and the dangers of poison gas. The Home Office Air Raid Precautions Department issued in 1935 *Air Raid Precautions Handbook No. 2*, which certainly pulled no punches in telling the public what they might expect. It contains detailed descriptions of the kinds of poison gas that might be used and their various effects. It continues with advice on the creation of hermetically-sealed environments and how to supply such refuges. The prevailing wisdom of the day is perhaps best summed up by John Langdon-Davies, in one of the boldest and most specific futurological essays of the 1930s, *A Short History of the Future* (1935). Number one in his series of twenty-three prophecies is this:

> War is ultimately inevitable. It will be fought by armies unable to protect civilian populations, against which, from the very first moment, all efforts of the attackers will be aimed. It will be short and involve inevitably the destruction of the governments of both victors and vanquished, if they can be shown either to have promoted it, or to have been criminally negligent in not preventing it.[12]

This was so completely taken for granted that many of the speculative fictions of the later 1930s go beyond simple alarmism and

FUTURE WARS, 1890-1950

graphic accounts of the horrors of war in order to indulge an intense bitterness, suggesting that the coming self-destruction of man is an ironically appropriate fate. This cynicism is seen in several different forms. John Gloag (who was actually invalided out of the Great War when he caught a lungful of mustard gas) produced *Winter's Youth* (1934), a black comedy in which one level-headed politician battles against the prevailing insanity of the day in the hope of preventing war; but cannot in the end prevent the cities of Europe being devastated by the new superweapon, "radiant inflammatol," as a result of the pig-headed incompetence and petty power games of aging statesmen. His later novel *Manna* describes the discovery of a magic mushroom which turns people into happy pacifists, but which has to be banned in order that the nations of Europe can get on with the serious business of war; to add to the irony the second world war actually broke out while this novel was in press.

In several novels, including *The One Sane Man* (1934) by Francis Beeding, the excellent *The Peacemaker* (1934) by C. S. Forester, and *I'll Blackmail the World* (1935) by Andrew Wood, lone inventors try to use new discoveries to blackmail the world into disarmament, but all are doomed to fail miserably as the security forces act quickly to preserve the freedom of self-destruction.

Perhaps the most remarkable of all these bitter novels is *Gay Hunter* (1934) by J. Leslie Mitchell. This is one more in the sequence of visions of a future world reduced to barbarism by all-out war, but in this story the return is no tragedy, but rather the perfect cure for a sick civilization. The eponymous heroine, shortly before she is catapulted into the future by a Dunnean experiment with time, reflects on the state of the world:

> What a world! Hellnblast, what a world!—as Daddy used to say in moments when it vexed him overmuch. The cruelty, the beastliness, the hopelessness of it. Not for herself...But she was only one, and a fortunate one....All the poor folk labouring at filthy jobs under the gathering clouds of war and an undreamed tyranny—what *had* they to live for? Even she herself—would she always escape? unless she hid from her kind in the busy world of men, sought out some little corner and abandoned life like the folk at Rainier, like the hermits of the Thebaid. Those children of hers—would they escape the wheels and wires of life any more than the children of others? Or their children thereafter, and so on and on, till the world was one great pounding machine, pounding the life out of humanity, making it an ant-like slave-crawl on an earth turned to a dunghill of its own futilities....

> Suddenly. the night outside seemed to crack. Sheet lightning flowed low and saffron down over Pewsey, lighting up the Downs, and flowing soft in the foliage of the trees...The earth looked a moment like a sea of fire, as though that Next War's bombardments were opening their barrage.13

Gay Hunter later learns that this world was eventually destroyed by atom bombs and poisonous dusts, to give way to an era of Fascist "Hierarchies" perpetually at war with one another. These conflicts continued until the contending forces were annihilated. She is accompanied into the new stone age by two British Fascists, who are intent on civilizing the innocent hunter-gatherers and rebuilding the old world, but she will not have it. Unlike Theodore Savage, who merely stood by while his world cultivated an obsessive hatred of science and its fruits, Gay Hunter takes arms against the forces of evil and saves the world for innocence and simplicity.

In the later 1930s the desperate fear of a new world war was complicated by the growing feeling that in spite of all the risks some kind of military action would eventually be necessary to contain and control Hitler. In 1935 S. Fowler Wright was commissioned by a newspaper proprietor to visit Germany and Czechoslovakia in order to investigate the new German state and offer prognostications as to the likely development of the European situation. In consequence he wrote *Prelude in Prague*, a novel about the outbreak of a new world war in 1938, begun by a German invasion of Czechoslovakia. Serialization of the story in the *Sunday Dispatch* created a minor sensation, and Wright was asked at one point by the Foreign Office to be careful of inserting anything in his next episode which would prejudice real negotiations with Hitler.

Prelude in Prague is, for most of its length, a conventional spy thriller, but in the final chapters it becomes something rather different as the bombing of Prague by German aircraft is described with a cold clinicality that brings home the horror of such an experience far more than any hysterical extravagance could have done. The same phenomenon is seen in Joseph O'Neill's *Day of Wrath* (1936), which begins as an execrable and hopelessly implausible yellow peril thriller, but is transformed in its climax, which features a flat description, drained of all emotion, of an England devastated by the customary explosives, incendiary bombs, and poison gases. The chilling matter-of-factness transcends the lack of conviction which mars the early chapters of the novel, signifying a numb acceptance of the inevitability of what is being described.

Fowler Wright followed up *Prelude in Prague* with two sequels, *Four Days War* (1936) and *Megiddo's Ridge* (1937), which chart the course of the new world war. The Americans come in on the side

FUTURE WARS, 1890-1950

of Britain, but the mainland of Europe has to be abandoned by the Allies, proving quite indefensible. The forces mass for a final confrontation in North Africa, and the suggestion is made—ironically, of course—that their climactic clash may well take place in the Middle East, close to the site of the Biblical Armageddon. Conventional issues are stressed—the unpreparedness of Britain, especially with respect to air power; the awesome destructive power of chemical weapons; the impossibility of England feeding even her surviving population from her own resources. The conventional "ending," however, comes at the end of the second volume rather than the third:

> Deliberately, he directed his mind to the larger issue: the problem that faced mankind. Would it find some basis of lasting peace? Or would it be entirely destroyed by its own wars? Or would it revert to some better barbarism, such as might be within the larger purpose of God, that men might commence anew? He saw that, even if no divine intervention came, the third question was the most likely to find an affirmative reply.
>
> For how could men hope to abolish war?
>
> It would not be done by denouncing it as something too dreadful to come, nor by appealing to fears or greeds.
>
> It would not be ended by force, though that might be the most plausible way: to organize a controlling tyranny to be called police, which might be just, till its rulers changed.
>
> It would not be ended by the humourless suggestion of Mr. H. G. Wells that the human race should become the abject slaves of the scientists whose inventions had already brought them so near to a final wreck.
>
> To abolish war, it would be necessary to change the natures and hearts of men.
>
> Could it be done in the Name which had been rejected by those who had now broken loose to subdue the world, and in that of the three-fold Cross which was the symbol of British power?
>
> It was hard to say. But, if not, it was clear that the civilization of Europe, if not of the whole world, must go down in a red twilight of blood....Which did not alter the present urgency of that which he had undertaken to do.[14]

OPENING MINDS, BY BRIAN STABLEFORD

The final sentence, though it appears trivial, is in fact significant. Many future war novels had ended with this kind of careless flurry of rhetorical questions, content with a summation of the basic issues at stake and an open query about the actual direction to be chosen. For Wright, that was no longer adequate; the time had come to go beyond that, even though there was nowhere to go. *Megiddo's Ridge* has an ending which is just as inconclusive, but there is no neat summary of the stakes and the opportunities. It ends in simple confusion, with the future unknown and unknowable. This was, perhaps, the most appropriate as well as the most honest ending available.

When the real war began, future war stories faded from the British literary scene, as was only to be expected. With the exception of a couple of propaganda pieces warning of the consequences of a Nazi victory, Britain produced no significant future war stories for some six years; the last to appear were Gloag's *Manna*, and Alfred Noyes's *The Last Man*, both published in 1940, but probably written before the outbreak of the war. The latter has the distinction of introducing the notion of a "doomsday weapon"—an ultimate deterrent to be used only in the last resort, which will destroy all life on earth in reprisal for an enemy attack. Needless to say, the book begins with the use of the weapon.

America, however, did not enter the war until December 1941, and the three-year period which saw the disappearance of British future war stories saw the first real emergence of American ones. Robert Nathan, in *They Went on Together* (1941), and Hendrik van Loon, in *Invasion* (1941), both imagined America invaded as European countries had been; but the most striking novels of the period offered images of Europe utterly devastated by the war. L. Ron Hubbard's *Final Blackout* (1940) was one of several dramatic future war stories to appear in the pulp science fiction magazines, but is outdone in extremism by *The Twenty-Fifth Hour* (1940) by Herbert Best. Here, the agricultural base of European society is so completely destroyed that its populations are atomized into a war of all against all. Armies disintegrate as communications break down, and every group of soldiers becomes a tiny army fighting anyone and everyone for the chance to survive. Men become predators hunting one another:

> From the first cannibalism was inevitable. The efficient social systems of the old world had made it possible for the farmer to feed many times his number of traders, manufacturers, carriers, distributors, people in the luxury trade and idle gentlefolk. Then, as farming became unsafe, there was a brief moment, a few months, at the most, of occasional surfeit, when livestock could be slaughtered, stores and storehouses filled. But soon mankind was forced to drop back

past the agricultural stage, past even the pastoral stage, to the dim, prehistoric age of hunters. Since wild animals were scarce in Europe, and the human animal unfitted in limb, lung, stomach and teeth, particularly in teeth, for hunting, he had fallen back upon the only source of food supply which existed in sufficient quantities: an animal, half dead, by comparison with other animals, half blind, almost lacking in the sense of smell, slow of movement, nearly defenceless; he could only prey upon his fellow-men.[15]

The novel also imagines the depopulation of America by bacteriological warfare, and in the end the only hope for a new rise to civilization is to be found in Africa—specifically, Egypt—where the story of civilization first began. The racism of Tracy, Shiel, and Waterloo is ironically inverted here: it is the Anglo-Saxons who are the losers, and the meeker, more primitive cultures are the inheritors of the earth.

The second world war was much less devastating than the anticipatory visions had suggested. In respect of chemical warfare the Geneva Convention held up; both sides stockpiled poison gases, including nerve gases, as a precautionary measure, but these were left unused. Of all the cities that were attacked by great fleets of bombers, only one was utterly destroyed: the German city of Dresden. London, although it was badly battered, survived the blitz to which it was subjected by the Luftwaffe. It was not that the war failed to produce horrors, but the horrors which it did produce were of an unexpected kind. Even S. Fowler Wright, who predicted in *Megiddo's Ridge* that the Nazis would set aside moral standards which had henceforth seemed inviolable, did not foresee concentration camps and gas chambers.

As far as further anticipations of war were concerned, however, the experience of the second world war was in no sense reassuring. In the manner of its ending, it reawakened all the desperate fears which had been exhibited in the most extreme of the earlier future war stories. Hiroshima and Nagasaki were destroyed, not by saturation bombing by great aerial fleets—one such fleet had already failed to destroy Tokyo—but by single planes carrying single bombs. Just at that point in time when it might have been possible to conclude that Wells, Hamilton, Mitchell, and Wright had protested too much, it was shown very clearly that, after all, they might have been right. The fact that the Nazis, even in the extremes of their desperation, had refrained from using poison gas suddenly seemed to be a hollow victory.

The pattern of future war stories following the end of World War II is sufficiently well-known not to require any elaboration here. Everyone has read, or seen, or heard accounts of the probable course of a nuclear war. Everyone is familiar with the proposition that such a war might smash civilization, and might well obliterate all life on the surface of the earth. Today, The *World Set Free* seems to be a tame and altogether unconvincing fantasy, and there is nothing particularly extreme about *Gay Hunter*. Atomic holocaust stories have spread the anxiety which was once unique to Western Europe throughout the world. In America, such stories were a new phenomenon, and tended to exhibit the moral concern and alarmist fervor which befits a newly-realized threat. In Britain, the imaginative impact of the atom bomb was merely an ironic epilogue to a story which had already been told for a generation. In some of the British stories of nuclear war and its aftermath, one sees the same kind of bitterness that marks many future war stories of the 1930s taken to its satirical extreme. The best example is perhaps to be found in Aldous Huxley's *Ape and Essence* (1949), in which a nuclear war is held by its survivors to be the final proof of the all-powerful Belial, whose worship has perforce replaced that of the ineffectual Yahweh and the gentle godling, Christ. The Arch-Vicar of the post-holocaust community reminds us that we should have realized this anyhow:

> "And remember this," he adds: "even without synthetic glanders, even without the atomic bomb, Belial could have achieved all His purposes. A little more slowly, perhaps, but just as surely, men would have destroyed themselves by destroying the world they lived in. They couldn't escape. He had them skewered on both His horns. If they managed to wriggle off the horn of total war, they would find themselves impaled on starvation. And if they were starving, they would be tempted to resort to war. And just in case they should try to find a peaceful and rational way out of their dilemma, He had another subtler horn of self-destruction all ready for them. From the very beginning of the industrial revolution He foresaw that men would be made so overwhelmingly bumptious by the miracles of their own technology that they would soon lose all sense of reality. And that's precisely what happened....
> "I tell you, my dear sir, an undevout historian is mad. The longer you study modern history, the more evidence you find of Belial's Guiding Hand."[16]

In this judgment, the actual course of the second world war is held to be irrelevant; the truth was to be found not in the events of the real world, but in the imaginings of the speculative writers: there had been, and could be, no salvation.

FUTURE WARS, 1890-1950

Future war stories are still being written, and will no doubt continue to be written until they come true. One can still see the same balance of documentary realism and visionary extravagance. The message has not altered now for more than a generation; the same questions remain open and there seems to be no hope of their imminent closure.

The first future war stories described in this essay, like the pioneering description of "The Battle of Dorking," were intended to excite the public imagination. They attempted to create anxiety where—it was assumed—there was an unjustified complacency. In the course of time, the visions of future war changed their role. They became reflections of an anxiety that was already widespread, trying (and failing) to find an appropriate response to that anxiety, feeding an alarmist appetite which has never diminished.

Now that we can look back on the actual course of World War II, there is a temptation to write off all the future war stories of the 1920s and 1930s as failed prophecies—accounts of wars to come which were quite simply proved wrong. This is, however, the wrong way to look at those stories. History could only take one path, but there is nothing predestined about that path, and things could have happened otherwise. In trying to evaluate the significance of yesterday's imaginary wars we must try to take into consideration not only the actual world war that broke out in 1939 and was ended in 1945, but also the wars that might have been. In a sense, the surprising thing is that the Geneva Convention did hold up, and that poison gases were never used. The images of future war produced in the 1930s cannot be devalued or invalidated simply because World War II was fought less viciously than it might have been.

It is tempting to suggest that just as the future war stories written before the Great War might have contributed to the eagerness with which the European powers launched themselves into that war, so the future war stories written after the Great War may have helped to make those same powers more careful and more scrupulous in the way they fought World War II. This remains, however, a matter for conjecture, just as it remains a matter for conjecture as to whether the future war stories written in the last fifty years might assist in some small measure in the averting of World War III. The contribution of real history to the anticipation of the future is obvious enough; the reverse is not at all obvious.

What should, however, be stressed is the fact that as private visions played out in the arena of inner space, images of future war cannot help but affect the way at least some individuals think, and plan, and pray. They can create, in the minds of some individuals, a sense of the fragility of civilization, of the exterminability of mankind. They can alter the way people see, feel, and act.

Such is the variability of human beings that there are probably many different ways in which individuals might be changed by the unwelcome revelations that images of future war force upon us. It is difficult to generalize, even speculatively, about what effects might be seen: panic, despair, and moral anaesthesia might be as likely products as passionate fervor in the cause of peace. Whatever the result of any such analysis might be, though, the fact remains that future war stories have become an instrument of contemporary thought—a heuristic device used by very many people as they try to figure out what their lives do and will amount to. It is in this context that we must explain their existence and evaluate their endeavors.

NOTES

CHAPTER ONE

[1] Marshall McLuhan, *Counterblast*. Toronto: McClelland & Stewart, 1968, p. 99.

CHAPTER TWO

[1] All quotes from William Wilson are taken from *A Little Earnest Book Upon a Great Old Subject*. London: Darton & Co. 1851, p. 131-149. I am indebted to John Eggeling, who first directed my attention to the existence of the book, and to the Scottish National Lending Library for letting me look at their copy of the book.
[2] Richard Henry Horne, who preferred to sign himself R. Hengist Horne, is perhaps best known for his collection of literary criticism, *A New Spirit of the Age*, published twenty years after Hazlitt's original. He lived an active life, fighting in the Mexican War against Spain and serving as commissioner for the crown lands in Australia for many years. He wrote criticisms, satire, and epic poetry, and employed a good many pseudonyms (he wrote a history of duelling as "Lucius O'Trigger"). *The Poor Artist* was reprinted in 1871, with some new speculative material added, but nevertheless seems to have escaped the notice of the SF bibliographers.
[3] The reference is to the Scottish poet Thomas Campbell, author of *The Pleasures of Hope* and *The Battle of the Baltic*.

CHAPTER FOUR

[1] *Science Wonder Quarterly* 1 (Winter 1930): 250+.
[2] Clifford D. Simak, *Ring Around the Sun*. New York: Simon & Schuster, 1953, p. 158.

CHAPTER FIVE

[1] George Bernard Shaw, *Back to Methuselah*. London: Constable, 1921, p. 260-266.
[2] Ernest Gellner, *Legitimation of Belief*. Cambridge: Cambridge University Press, 1975, p. 61-62.

OPENING MINDS, BY BRIAN STABLEFORD

3Theodore Sturgeon, *More Than Human*. New York: Farrar, Straus, & Young, 1953, p. 185-186.

CHAPTER SIX

1Geoffrey Dennis, *The End of the World*. London: Eyre & Spottiswoode, 1930, p. 178-179.
2Samuel Butler, *Erewhon*, Chapter XXV.
3Erskine Childers, *The Riddle of the Sands*. 1931.

CHAPTER EIGHT

1Karl R. Popper, *The Poverty of Historicism*. London: Routledge & Kegan Paul, 1957, p. iv.
2*Ibid.* p. 105+.
3Karl R. Popper, *The Open Society and Its Enemies*. London: Routledge & Kegan Paul, 1945, vol. 2, p. 197.
4Karl Marx, *Capital*. London: Penguin Books, 1976, vol. 1, p. 92. Quoted in *The Open Society and Its Enemies*, vol. 2, p. 86.
5See Friedrich Engels's essay, "Socialism: Utopian and Scientific," and the attack on Proudhon in *The Poverty of Philosophy* (whose title, of course, inspired the title of Popper's exercise in table-turning).
6*The Poverty of Historicism*, p. v-vii.
7Karl Marx, *Selected Writings*, edited by D. McLellan. Oxford: Oxford University Press, 1977, p. 202.
8William H. Shaw, *Marx's Theory of History*. London: Hutchinson, 1978.
9Angus Walker, *Marx: His Theory and Its Context*. London: Longman, 1978.
10*Capital*, p. 307+.
11*Ibid.* p. 307+ and 492+, especially p. 509.
12*The Poverty of Historicism*, p. 13-15.
13*The Open Society and Its Enemies*, vol. 2, p. 198.
14*Capital*, p. 929.

CHAPTER NINE

1George Griffith, *The Angel of the Revolution*. London: Tower Publishing Co., 1893, p. 390-391.
2Louis Tracy, *The Final War*. London: C. Arthur Pearson, 1896, p. 370-371.
3Stanley Waterloo, *Armageddon*. Chicago & New York: Rand, McNally & Co., 1898, p. 257-259.
4Edward Shanks, *The People of the Ruins*. London: William Collins, 1920, p. 290.

NOTES

[5] Cicely Hamilton, *Theodore Savage*. London: Leonard Parsons, 1922, p. 289-290.
[6] *Ibid.*, p. 315.
[7] *Ibid.*, p. 319-320.
[8] Winston Churchill, "Shall We Commit Suicide?" quoted in *Janus; or, The Conquest of War*, by William McDougall. London: Kegan Paul, Trench, Trübner, 1925, p. 23-24.
[9] *Ibid.*, p. 25.
[10] J. B. S. Haldane, *Callinicus: A Defence of Chemical Warfare*. London: Kegan Paul, Trench, Trübner, 1925, p. 10-11.
[11] Stanley Baldwin, Speech in the House of Commons, 10 November 1932, quoted in *Invasion from the Air*, by Frank McIlraith and Roy Connolly. London: Grayson & Grayson, 1934, p. 5.
[12] John Langdon-Davies, *A Short History of the Future*. London: George Routledge, 1935, p. 84.
[13] J. Leslie Mitchell, *Gay Hunter*. London: Heinemann, 1934, p. 22-23.
[14] S. Fowler Wright, *Four Days War*. London: Robert Hale, 1936, p. 287-288.
[15] Herbert Best, *The Twenty-Fifth Hour*. London: Jonathan Cape, 1940, p. 170.
[16] Aldous Huxley, *Ape and Essence*. London: Chatto & Windus, 1949.

SELECTED BIBLIOGRAPHY

Baldwin, Stanley. Speech in House of Commons, 10 November 1932. Quoted in *Invasion from the Air*, by Frank McIlraith and Roy Connolly. London: Grayson & Grayson, 1934.
Best, Herbert. *The Twenty-Fifth Hour*. London: Jonathan Cape, 1940.
Churchill, Winston. "Shall We Commit Suicide?" in *Nash's Pall Mall Magazine* (September 1924). Quoted in *Janus; or, the Conquest of War*, by William McDougall. London: Kegan Paul, Trench, Trübner, 1925.
Clarke, I. F. *Voices Prophesying War 1763-1984*. Oxford: Oxford University Press, 1966.
Gloag, John. *Manna*. London: Cassell, 1940.
Gloag, John. *Tomorrow's Yesterday*. London: George Allen & Unwin, 1932.
Gloag, John. *Winter's Youth*. London: George Allen & Unwin, 1934.
Griffith, George. *The Angel of the Revolution*. London: Tower Publishing Co., 1893.
Haldane, J. B. S. *Callinicus: A Defence of Chemical Warfare*. London: Kegan Paul, Trench, Trübner, 1925.
Hamilton, Cicely. *Theodore Savage*. London: Leonard Parsons, 1922.
Huxley, Aldous. *Ape and Essence*. London: Chatto & Windus, 1949.
Langdon-Davies, John. *A Short History of the Future*. London: George Routledge, 1935.
Le Queux, William. *The Great War in England in 1897*. London: Tower Publishing Co., 1894.
Le Queux, William. *The Invasion of 1910*. London: Nash, 1906.
Mitchell, J. Leslie. *Gay Hunter*. London: William Heinemann, 1934.
Moorcock, Michael. "Introduction" to *Before Armageddon* and *England Invaded*. London: George Allen & Unwin, 1975 and 1977.
Newton, W. Douglas. *War*. London: Methuen, 1914.
Noyes, Alfred. *The Last Man*. London: Murray, 1940.
O'Neill, Joseph. *Day of Wrath*. London: Victor Gollancz, 1936.
Shanks, Edward. *The People of the Ruins*. London: William Collins, 1920.
Shiel, M. P. *The Dragon*. London: Grant Richards, 1913.
Shiel, M. P. *The Yellow Danger*. London: Grant Richards, 1898.
Tracy, Louis. *The Final War*. London: C. Arthur Pearson, 1896.
Waterloo, Stanley. *Armageddon*. Chicago & New York: Rand, McNally, & Co., 1898.
Wells, H. G. *Anticipations of the Reaction of Mechanical and Scientific Progress Upon Human Life and Thought*. London: Chapman & Hall, 1901.
Wells, H. G. *The War in the Air*. London: Bell, 1908.
Wells, H. G. *The World Set Free*. London: Macmillan, 1914.
Wright, S. Fowler. *Four Days War*. London: Robert Hale, 1936.
Wright, S. Fowler. *Megiddo's Ridge*. London: Robert Hale, 1937.
Wright, S. Fowler. *Prelude in Prague: A Story of the War of 1938*. London: Robert Hale, 1935.

INDEX

334, 34
A for Anything, 72-73
The Absolute at Large, 70
"Adam and No Eve," 76
The Adventure of Wyndham Smith, 64
After London, 58
After Utopia, 65
Against the Fall of Night, 43
"Age of Anxiety," 57-62
Air Raid Precautions Handbook, 126
"Alas, All Thinking!," 43, 68
Aldiss, Brian W., 58
Álfvén, Hannes, 71
All Aboard for Ararat, 55
Amazing Stories, 5, 18, 31, 70
"Ames" room, 91, 94
Anderson, Carl David, 27
Anderson, Poul, 26
Anders, Gunther, 78
The Angel of the Revolution, 60-61, 112-114, 116-117
animation, 92
Answers to Correspondents, 114
Anticipations, 116-117
Ape and Essence, 77, 132
The Ape of London, 44
Ardrey, Robert, 67
Armageddon, 57, 76-77, 115-116
"As Far as Thought Can Reach," 40
Asimov, Isaac, 26, 33-34, 67, 70-71
"Autofac," 70
"Avatar," 45
Azandes, 54, 56
Back to Methuselah, 40-41, 47
Bagehot, Walter, 30
Baldwin, Stanley, 125
Bates, Harry, 43, 68
"Bathe Your Bearings in Blood," 69
"The Battle of Dorking," 60, 111-112, 117, 125-126, 133
Bayley, Barrington J., 26
Becquerel, Antoine Henri, 62
Beeding, Francis, 127
"The Bell-Tower," 58
Bell, Neil, 76, 122
Bellamy, Edward, 31, 35, 39, 59
Benson, Robert Hugh, 118
Beresford, John, 55
Bergson, Henri, 23-24, 41
Best, Herbert, 130-131
The Best of Science Fiction, 101
Bester, Alfred, 76
"Beyond Bedlam," 104

"The Big Flash," 57, 77
"The Big Space Fuck," 84
"The Big Trip Up Yonder," 81, 102
Black, Ladbroke, 76, 122
Black and White, 112
The Black Death, 76, 122
Blake of the Rattlesnake, 114
Blind Voices, 47
"Blindness," 107
Blish, James, 26, 34, 43, 50, 78, 81-82, 104
Bloch, Robert, 69
Bohr, Niels, 22
"The Book of the Machines," 58, 68
Brackett, Leigh, 45
Bradbury, Ray, 43
The Brain Stealers, 44, 46
Brainrack, 82
Brave New World, 32, 69, 77, 109, 132
Breuer, Miles J., 70, 76
The Broken Trident, 125-126
Brunner, John, 34-35, 81-83, 102
Buckle, Henry Thomas, 31
Bunyan, John, 29
Butler, Octavia, 47
Butler, Samuel, 58, 68
Buzzati, Dino, 71
By Furies Possessed, 45-46
Caesar's Column, 59, 106
Callinicus..., 124
Camp Concentration, 34
Campbell, John W., Jr., 26, 32, 43-44, 68, 77, 101, 107
Campbell, Thomas, 18
A Canticle for Leibowitz, 77
Capek, Karel, 70
Capital—SEE: *Das Kapital*
"The Captain of the Mary Rose," 112, 114
Carson, Rachel, 82
Cartesian dualism, 39, 41-42, 44-47, 50, 95, 97
Cartmill, Cleve, 107
The Castle Keeps, 85
"Catastrophe à la Mode," 80-85
"catastrophe fiction," 53-90
"Cathedrals in Space," 50, 78
Cat's Cradle, 86
"Cellarius," 58
"The Census Takers," 81
"Centre for the Study of Metaphor," 6
Chaos, 126

139

Chesney, George, 60, 111-112
Chesterton, G. K., 102-103
Childers, Erskine, 75, 118
Childhood's End, 33, 43-44, 48
Children of the Atom, 33
Churchill, Winston, 122-123, 125
Cities in Flight, 34
The City and the Stars, 43
"The City of the Living Dead," 64-65, 68
Clarke, Arthur C., 26, 33-34, 43-44, 48
Clarke, I. F., 111-134
Clement, Hal, 26, 45
"clinamen," 26
Clowes, W. Laird, 112
Club of Rome, 83
Coblentz, Stanton A., 76
The Collapse of Homo Sapiens, 75-76, 122
Colomb, P. H., 112
Colossus, 71
Communist Manifesto, 108
Compton, D. G., 81
"The Concept of Mind in Science Fiction," 6, 37-51
Condorcet, Marquis de, 30
Conklin, Groff, 101
Connolly, Roy, 126
Corelli, Marie, 40
The Crack of Doom, 61
Crisp, Frank, 44
Cromie, Robert, 61
"The Crucifixion of Christ Considered as an Uphill Bicycle Race," 25
Daily Mail, 117
Dalton, Moray, 76, 122
"Dancers at the End of Time," 66
"Danger!," 118
Darwinism, 23, 30, 32, 41, 56, 61, 63, 104, 114
"Darwin among the Machines," 58
Davis, Gerry, 82
Dawson, A. J., 118
Day of Wrath, 76, 128
de Camp, L. Sprague, 77
De Rerum Natura, 26
"Deadline," 107
Delivrez Prométhée, 84
Democritus, 26
Dennis, Geoffrey, 62-63
Descartes, René, 39
Deshusses, Jérôme, 84
Desmond, Shaw, 76, 122, 126
The Devil Takes a Holiday, 55
Dianetics, 21-22
Dick, Philip K., 26, 70-71, 81
Dirac, Paul Adrien, 27
Disch, Thomas M., 34, 83
Donaldson, Stephen R., 97
Donnelly, Ignatius, 59, 106
Doorways in the Sand, 46
Douglas Duane, 45
Doyle, Arthur Conan, 45, 118
Dr. Berkeley's Discovery, 39

Dr. Heidenhoff's Process, 39
Dr. Jekyll and Mr. Hyde, 39
Dr. Strangelove, 77, 80
The Dragon, 117
The Dragons of Eden, 68
The Dreaming Earth, 35
Dunne, John William, 127
Dunsany, Lord, 69-70
The Dynamics of Creation, 5
"E for Effort," 32, 72-73
"Ecocatastrophe!," 83
Economic and Philosophical Manuscripts, 105-106
Eddington, Arthur Stanley, 27
Edison, Thomas Alva, 24, 106
Ehrlich, Paul, 83
Einstein, Albert, 22, 27, 104
Eliot, T. S., 78
Ellison, Harlan, 26, 71
Elwood, Roger, 84
The End of All Songs, 66
The End of Eternity, 33
The End of the Dream, 34, 82
The End of the World, 6, 62-63
Engels, Friedrich, 30, 102
The Engineer, 112
The English Utopia, 64
Epicurus, 26
"Épimetheus Unbound," 69-74
"The Equalizer," 73
Erewhon, 58, 68
Escher, M. C., 91
"An Essay on the Principle of Population," 80, 100-101
"The Eternal Adam," 121-122
The Exploits and Opinions of Dr. Faustroll, 25
Famous Fantastic Mysteries, 57
Farmer, Philip José, 45
Farrère, Claude, 106
Fawcett, Edward Douglas, 59, 114
Fawcett, Edgar, 39-40, 45
Feuerbach, Ludwig, 105
Final Blackout, 76, 130
The Final War, 114-115
Finney, Jack, 44
The First Men in the Moon, 24
Flammarion, Camille, 40
Flecker, James Elroy, 64
Forester, C. S., 127
Forster, E. M., 32, 64
Four Days War, 128-130
France, Anatole, 106
Frankenstein, 58
"Frankenstein Syndrome," 70
"future shock," 83
"Future Wars," 6, 111-134
Galbraith, John Kenneth, 106-107
The Gas War..., 76, 122
Gautier, Théophile, 45
Gay Hunter, 127-128, 132
Gellner, Ernest, 42-43
Geneva Convention, 124, 131, 133
George, Peter, 77

INDEX

Gernsback, Hugo, 15, 18-19, 21-22, 31-32, 35, 70, 99
gestalt, 48-50
"ghost in the machine," 42
The Ghost of Guy Thyrle, 40
Gloag, John, 76, 122, 127, 130
God Bless You, Mr. Rosewater, 86
The Gods Hate Kansas, 44, 46
Godwin, William, 30, 34, 80, 101
Gollancz, Victor, 24
"The Gostak and the Doshes," 76
Graham, P. Anderson, 75-76, 122
The Great Computer, 71
"The Great Keinplatz Experiment," 45
The Great War in England in 1897, 114
The Great War of 189-, 112
"The Great War of 1892," 112
The Great War Syndicate, 115
Greenberg, Martin H., 6
Griffith, George, 60-62, 112-114, 116-119
Griffith, Mary, 17
Grimm's law, 100
Guin, Wyman, 104
Gunn, James E., 65
Habermas, Jürgen, 104
Haeckel, Ernst Heinrich, 41, 100
Hague Convention, 123-124
Halcyon Drift, 45-46
Haldane, J. B. S., 18, 124
Hamilton, Cicely, 120-121, 131
Harmsworth, Alfred, 117
Harness, Charles L., 34-35
Harper, Vincent, 37-39, 41
Harrison, Harry, 34, 81
Hartmann the Anarchist, 59, 114
Heinlein, Robert A., 26, 44-46, 102
Heisenberg, August, 26
Helmholtz, Hermann von, 39
Herodotus, 64
Hertz, Heinrich Rudolph, 24, 27
Heuer, Kenneth, 63
Hidden World—SEE: *In Caverns Below*
His Wisdom, the Defender, 61
"The Hollow Men," 78
Horne, Richard Henry, 17, 22
"How to Construct a Time Machine," 23
Hubbard, L. Ron, 22, 76, 130
Hubble, Edwin Powell, 22
Hunt, Leigh, 17-18
Huxley, Aldous, 32, 69, 77, 88, 132
Huxley, Thomas Henry, 23
"I Have No Mouth and I Must Scream," 71
I Will Fear No Evil, 45-46
"Icarus; or, The Future of Science," 32
"If This goes On...," 102
I'll Blackmail the World, 127
The Immortal Error, 45
Immortality Inc., 45
In Caverns Below, 76

The Infinite Cage, 48
"Into the 28th Century," 31
Invasion, 130
Invasion from the Air, 126
The Invasion of 1910, 117, 119
Invasion of the Body-Snatchers, 44
The Invisible Man, 24
The Iron Dream, 77
"Is Civilization Doomed?," 63
The Island of Dr. Moreau, 24
"It Happened Tomorrow," 69
Jane, Fred T., 114
Jane's Fighting Ships, etc., 114
Jarry, Alfred, 23-28
Jefferies, Richard, 58
Joad, Cyril Edwin Mitchinson, 63, 84
Johannesson, Olaf—SEE: Alfvén, Hannes
Johnson, George Clayton, 81
Jones, D. F., 71
The Joy Makers, 65-66, 68
"Judgment Day," 77
Kahn, Herman, 83
Kant, Immanuel, 95
Das Kapital, 102, 106
Keller, David H., 68
Kelvin, William Thompson, 24, 26
Kidd, Virginia, 84
Knight, Damon, 45, 72-73
Knight, Norman L., 81
Köhler, Wolfgang, 48
Kornbluth, Cyril M., 33, 81-82
Lafferty, R. A., 26
Laing, R. D., 5
Lamarck, Jean Baptiste de, 41, 68
"The Land Ironclads," 116
The Land of Cokaygne, 64-65
Langdon-Davies, John, 126
Larger than Life, 71
"The Last Generation," 64
The Last Great Naval War, 112
The Last Man, 55, 76, 130
"The Last Question," 71
The Last Revolution, 69-70
Laumer, Keith, 48
Le Queux, William, 113-114, 117, 119
Leinster, Murray, 44, 71
Lest Ye Die—SEE: *Theodore Savage*
Level 7, 77
"The Life and Times of Multivac," 67
The Limits to Growth, 83
A Little Earnest Book..., 15-16, 22
Logan's Run, 81
"A Logic Named Joe," 71
The Long Loud Silence, 77
Looking Backward..., 31, 35, 59
The Lord of Labor, 117
Lorraine, Lilith, 31
"The Lost Continent," 82
"The Lotus Eaters," 62-69
Lovecraft, H. P., 72
Lumen, 40
"The Machine Stops," 32, 64
McIlraith, Frank, 126

141

McLaughlin, Dean, 82
McLuhan, Marshall, 5, 9, 12
Make Room! Make Room!, 34, 81
Malthus, Thomas Robert, 30, 34, 80, 82-83, 100-102
"The Man of the Year Million," 43, 68
Manna, 127, 130
Manning, Laurence, 64-65
Manuel, Frank, 79
"The Marching Morons," 81
Marconi, Guglielmo, 62
Marx, Karl, 30, 32, 59, 73, 99-110
"Marxism, Science Fiction, and the Poverty of Prophecy," 6, 99-110
Master of Life and Death, 81
Maxwell, James Clerk, 22, 24, 27, 39-40
Mechasm, 70
Megiddo's Ridge, 128-131
Melville, Herman, 58
"The Menagerie," 66
Mendel, Gregor Johann, 63
Merril, Judith, 77
The Message, 118
"Metamorphosite," 43
Métaphors, 6
"Miles"—SEE: Bell, Neil
Millard, Joseph J., 44
Miller, Walter M., 77
Mind at the End of its Tether, 31
Mind of My Mind, 47
Mind Switch, 45
Mr. Britling Sees It Through, 74
Mitchell, J. Leslie, 127-128, 131
A Modern Utopia, 63
Moorcock, Michael, 66
More Than Human, 48
Morris, Desmond, 68
Morris, William, 31-32, 58-59
The Mortgage on the Brain, 37-39
Morton, A. L., 64
Mother Night, 86
Müller, Johann, 39
Munro, H. H.—SEE: Saki
Mystery of Evelyn Delorme, 39
"The Mythology of Man-Made Catastrophe," 6, 53-90
"The Naked Sky," 65
The Napoleon of Notting Hill, 102-103
Nathan, Robert, 130
Needle, 45
"A Negligible Experiment," 55
The New Industrial State, 106
The New Moon, 119
The New Nero, 39
New Wave, 26
Newcomb, Simon, 61
News from Nowhere, 31, 58
Newton, W. Douglas, 118-119
Nicolson, Harold, 107
"Night," 68
Nightmare Age, 83
Nineteen Eighty-Four, 32, 99, 109
Niven, Larry, 66
Noah, 55

Nolan, William F., 81
Noyes, Alfred, 55, 76, 130
Odysseus, 64
"Oedipus effect," 108-110
Offutt, Andrew J., 85
Olander, Joseph P., 6
Olds, James, 65
Olga Romanoff, 113, 117
On the Beach, 77
"On the Conservation of Force," 39
The One Sane Man, 127
O'Neill, Joseph, 76, 128
Onions, Oliver, 119
The Open Society..., 99-110
"Opening Minds," 23-28
Oppenheimer, J. Robert, 86
The Origin of Species, 31
Orwell, George, 32, 99
The Outlaws of the Air, 114
Paine, Albert Bigelow, 39
Pall Mall Magazine, 122
"Pandora's Millions," 72
Panshin, Alexei, 26
Paradise and Iron, 70, 73
The Paradox Men, 34
"Passengers," 44
Pataphysics, 25
The Peacemaker, 127
Pearson, C. Arthur, 111, 114-115
Pearson's Weekly, 112, 114
Pedler, Kit, 82
Pemberton, Max, 118
The People of the Ruins, 75, 119-120
Phenomenon of Man, 48
The Pilgrim's Progress, 29
Platt, Fletcher, 64-65
"The Plausibility of the Impossible," 6, 91-98
Pliny, 64
Player Piano, 32
Poe, Edgar Allan, 17, 19
Poetry of Science, 15-19, 22
Pogo, 85
Pohl, Frederik, 33, 44, 81, 83
Poincaré, Jules Henri, 24
The Poison War, 76, 122
"The Poisoned Bullet," 114
The Politics of Experience, 5
The Poor Artist, 17-19
Popper, Karl R., 99-110
"Possible Worlds," 18
Pournelle, Jerry, 66
The Poverty of Historicism, 100-110
The Poverty of Philosophy, 105
Pratt, Cornelia Atwood, 39
Prelude in Prague, 128
"The Pre-Persons," 81
Pro Patria, 118
"psi powers," 47, 93
"Psychology and Science Fiction," 6
Public Faces, 107
The Puppet Masters, 44, 46
The Quality of Mercy, 81
Rabkin, Eric, 6
Ragnarok, 76

INDEX

Reamy, Tom, 47
"The Rediscovery of the Unique," 25
The Reproductive System, 70
"The Revolt of the Pedestrians," 68
Reynolds, Mack, 35, 65-66
Rhine, Joseph Banks, 47
The Riddle of the Sands, 75, 118
Ring Around the Sun, 33
Roberts, Frederick Sleigh, 117, 119
A Romance of Two Worlds, 40
Röntgen, Wilhelm Conrad, 62
The Rose, 35
Roshwald, Mordecai, 77
Rossiter, Oscar, 48
Rousseau, Jean Jacques, 30, 32
The Ruins of Earth, 83
R.U.R., 70
Russell, Bertrand, 32
Russell, Eric Frank, 43-44
Rutherford, Ernest, 40
Ryle, Gilbert, 39, 41-42
Sagan, Carl, 68
St. Matthew, 53
Saki, 118
The Salvaging of Civilization, 74
Saving Worlds, 83-84
"Schizoid Science Fiction," 5
Science Fantasy, 5
"Science Fiction and the Mythology of Progress," 6, 29-35
Seaforth, A. N., 112
The Second Trip, 45
Secondary Worlds, 97
"SF: The Nature of the Medium," 5, 9-14
Shadow on the Hearth, 77
"Shall We Commit Suicide?," 122-123
Shanks, Edward, 75, 119-120
Shapley, Harlow, 22
"Shark Ship," 82
Shaw, George Bernard, 40-41, 43-44
Shaw, William H., 105
Sheckley, Robert, 45
The Sheep Look Up, 34, 82-83
Shelley, Mary, 58
Sherred, T. L., 32, 72
Shiel, M. P., 61, 115, 131
Shiras, Wilmar H., 33
The Shockwave Rider, 83
A Short History of the Future, 126
Short Stories, 115
Shute, Nevil, 77
Sibson, Francis, 76
Silent Spring, 82
Silverberg, Robert, 35, 44-45, 81, 84, 102
Simak, Clifford D., 33, 69, 104
Sinister Barrier, 44, 46
"Skirmish," 69
Sladek, John, 70
Slaughterhouse-5, 86
Slee, Richard, 39
Smith, George O., 72
Soddy, Frederick, 40
Son of Man, 35
The Space Merchants, 33, 79
Spanner, E. F., 125-126
Spencer, Herbert, 103
Spengler, Oswald, 34
Spinoza, Baruch, 95
Spinrad, Norman, 57, 77, 82
"Spirals," 66
Stand on Zanzibar, 34, 81, 83, 102
The Star Dwellers, 43
Star Trek, 66
The Stardroppers, 35
Starmind, 45
"Stenographers' Hands," 68
Stockton, Frank R., 115
The Stone That Never Came Down, 35
The Strand, 112, 118
Stuart, Don A.—SEE: Campbell, John W., Jr.
Sturgeon, Theodore, 33, 48, 78
Sunday Dispatch, 128
The Supermale, 24-25
"Surface Tension," 104
Suvin, Darko, 106
Sword of Rhiannon, 45
The Tale of the Big Computer, 71
"Target Generation," 104
Teilhard de Chardin, Pierre, 44, 48
Tetrasomy Two, 48
"theatre of the absurd," 25
Theodore Savage, 120-121, 128
They Went on Together, 130
This Mortal Coil, 45
"Thomas Covenant" stories, 97
Three Hundred Years Hence, 17
"Through the Horn of the the Ivory Gate," 106
"Thunder and Roses," 78
The Time Machine, 23, 63
Tiptree, James, Jr., 45
Titus Lucretius, 26
To Live Again, 45-46
Today and Tomorrow, 63
Toffler, Alvin, 83
Tolkien, J. R. R., 97
"Tomorrow and Tomorrow..."—SEE: "The Big Trip..."
Tomorrow's Yesterday, 76, 122
A Torrent of Faces, 81
The Tower, 119
Toynbee, Arnold, 34
Tracy, Louis, 114-115, 119, 131
Traitor to the Living, 45
"The Transcendental Voyage...," 5
Trevor, Elleston, 45
Tucker, Wilson, 77
Tung, Lee, 81
Turgot, Anne Robert Jacques, 29-30
The Twenty-Fifth Hour, 130-131
"Twilight," 32, 43, 68-69
Ubu Roi, 25
The Undying Fire, 55
"United Planets," 66
Unthinkable, 76
Up the Walls of the World, 45
Useless Hands, 106

143

Valiant Clay—SEE: *The Gas War...*
Van Arnam, Dave, 45
van Loon, Hendrik Willem, 130
van Vogt, A. E., 26
Vector, 6
Verne, Jules, 19, 21, 121-122
Victorian Science Fiction..., 106
Voices Prophesying War, 111-134
von Hanstein, Otfrid, 31
Vonnegut, Kurt, 32, 81, 84, 86, 102
Voyages Extraordinaires, 21
Voyages: Scenarios..., 83
The Vril Staff, 61
Vulcan's Hammer, 71
Walker, Angus, 105
War, 118-119
The War in the Air, 74, 116-119
The War of the Worlds, 24
"The War That Will End War," 74
Warren, J. Russell, 45
"Watchman," 119
Waterloo, Stanley, 115-117, 131
"We All Die Naked," 82
"We Programmed People," 44
"Weapons Too Dreadful...," 74-80
Wells, H. G., 23-28, 31, 43, 55, 61, 63, 68, 74, 88-89, 107, 116-119, 129, 131
Wertheimer, Leo, 48
"What Is Sin?," 86-90
When the Sleeper Wakes, 61, 116
"When We Went to See the End of the World," 84
When William Came, 118
White, Ted, 5, 45-46
The White Stone, 106
"Who Goes There?," 44
"William Wilson's Prospectus...," 15-22
Williamson, Jack, 71, 73
Wilson, William, 15-22
The Wind Obeys Lama Toru, 81
Winter's Youth, 127
"With Folded Hands," 71
Wollheim, Donald A., 5
Wood, Andrew, 127
The World Inside, 81, 102
The World Set Free, 74, 107, 117, 119
The Wounded Planet—SEE: *Saving Worlds*
Wright, S. Fowler, 64, 128-131
Wright brothers, 116
Wylie, Philip, 34, 82
"X.Y.Z.," 61
The Yellow Danger, 61, 115, 117
The Yellow Peril—SEE: *The Dragon*
Young, Edward, 29
Zelazny, Roger, 45

www.ingramcontent.com/pod-product-compliance
Ingram Content Group UK Ltd.
Pitfield, Milton Keynes, MK11 3LW, UK
UKHW041448180426
11946UKWH00001B/6